Contents

WOMEN
OF THE WARS OF THE ROSES

Jacquetta Woodville, Margaret of Anjou & Cecily Neville

Facebook page:

www.facebook.com/theforgottentudorwomen

Twitter:

https://twitter.com/SylviaBSo

Editorial services: Jennifer Quinlan
http://historicaleditorial.blogspot.com/

ISBN: 9798640899191

This book is dedicated to my daughter, Amanda, who makes me proud every day.

INTRODUCTION: WOMEN BEHIND THE WARS OF THE ROSES

Jacquetta Woodville, Margaret of Anjou and Cecily Neville are among the best-known female figures during the Wars of the Roses, a dynastic conflict that raged in England from 1455 to 1485. Jacquetta, daughter of the Count of Saint-Pol, married John Plantagenet of Lancaster, Duke of Bedford, and became one of the highest-ranking women in England and France. After Bedford's death, she married Sir Richard Woodville, a mere knight and squire, with whom she produced a large brood of children, including Elizabeth, the future Queen consort.

In her lifetime, Jacquetta was best known as the mother of Elizabeth Woodville, a commoner who married King Edward IV. In her afterlife, she is best known as the heroine in Philippa Gregory's bestselling novels of *The Cousins' War* series, *The Lady of the Rivers* and *The White Queen*, wherein she is depicted as an intelligent, strong woman with psychic abilities. Portrayed on screen by Janet

McTeer, Jacquetta became one of the most beloved characters in *The White Queen*.

Yet the real Jacquetta, a woman who was the mother and grandmother of kings and queens, is buried beneath a thick layer of myths. Was she really a witch, as suggested by contemporary rumours and modern fiction? Did she have a sinister influence of her son-in-law, Edward IV? Was she really a power-thirsty individual who sought the advancement of her family at all costs? Jacquetta is an elusive historical figure, but her importance cannot be emphasised enough. Through the marriage of her daughter to Edward IV, she is the ancestress of entire houses of royals: Elizabeth of York, Henry VIII, Margaret and Mary Tudor, Edward VI, Mary and Elizabeth Tudor and many, many more. Her blood flows through the veins of modern royalty, and it's only fitting that Jacquetta should become the subject of a biography.

Jacquetta's story is inevitably linked to the lives of two other women: Margaret of Anjou, Queen of England, and Cecily Neville, Duchess of York. In 1445, fifteen-year-old Margaret of Anjou made the perilous sea journey from France to England, where she married King Henry VI. Jacquetta was among the noble ladies selected to welcome Margaret and escort her from France to England. Soon

Jacquetta became one of Margaret's favourite ladies-in-waiting and chief confidante. The Queen's failure to provide a male heir, as well as her part in ceding French territories to her husband's political enemies, gained her many enemies among the nobility and general populace. When she finally gave birth to a son in 1453, her world came to a crashing halt.

In 1453, shortly before Margaret gave birth, Henry VI descended into a mysterious mental illness. Richard, Duke of York, who had hitherto been denied an important role in the government, seized the opportunity and became lord protector. But this powerful lord's ambitions clashed with Margaret of Anjou's own plans. As her husband rebelled against Henry VI, Cecily Neville, Duchess of York, found herself in the position of queen-to-be. England slid into chaos and war.

Set against the rich background of fifteenth-century court life are the interwoven stories of these three women whose relationships were tested by the changing loyalties of their husbands, sons and daughters.

CHAPTER 1:
A COUNT'S DAUGHTER

Jacquetta was born c. 1415 as the first daughter of Pierre I of Luxembourg, Count of Saint-Pol, Brienne and Conversano, and Margaret of Baux, daughter of Francesco, Duke of Andrea, and Sveva Orsini. On her mother's side, Jacquetta descended from Simon de Montfort, sixth Earl of Leicester, and Eleanor, daughter of King John of England. She thus had French, Italian and English noble blood flowing in her veins. Although precious little is known about Jacquetta's early years, it is possible to reconstruct them based on our knowledge of fifteenth-century childhood and the ideals medieval maidens were taught and encouraged to emulate.

Jacquetta's early days were spent with her wet nurse since noblewomen were encouraged not to breastfeed in order to regain their fertility quickly. In 1418, Jacquetta was joined in the nursery by her brother Louis, who would eventually succeed their father as Count of Saint-Pol. Six more children were born to the count and countess: Theobald, Jacques, Valeran, Jean, Catherine and Isabelle. Jacquetta's father ruled over vast territories located in France and Italy. Besides his title of Count of Saint-Pol, Brienne and Conversano, he was also Lord of Enghien, a town located in the province of Hainault, where Jacquetta grew up. The children were brought up together until about the age of six, when boys and girls were separated to pursue different strands of education. Mothers, although they didn't teach their children directly, were responsible for directing and supervising their schooling.

The lives of fifteenth-century noblewomen were shaped by manuals written by Christine de Pisan, who was hailed, then as now, as "one of the most remarkable and respected literary figures in the courts of Europe".[1] Born in 1365 in Venice, Christine left Italy with her family and travelled to the court of Charles V of France, where her father acquired a position as the King's physician and astrologer. Christine married when she was fifteen years old; her fortunes changed dramatically when Charles V's death demoted her father from his prominent court post and then again when she became a widow in 1390. With family to support, Christine became a professional writer and managed to attract high-profile patrons, such as the Duke of Burgundy and King of France. Christine is best remembered for defending women in *The Book of the City of*

Ladies and *The Treasure of the City of Ladies.* Her books offered advice for princesses and noblewomen and were thus highly popular. Later in her life, Jacquetta owned one of Christine's books. Jacquetta's ownership of the book can be established without doubt; she inscribed her name, "Jaquette", and inserted a personal motto, "sour tous autres", meaning "above all others", in the outer margin of Christine's *Epistre au Dieu d'Amours.*[2]

Christine explained that "the wise lady who loves her children dearly will be diligent about their education", ensuring that "they will learn first of all to serve God, and to read and write, and that the teacher will be careful to make them learn their prayers well".[3] Besides her native language, which was French, Jacquetta probably learned Latin, as Christine de Pisan encouraged mothers to persuade fathers that children should have rudimentary knowledge of that language. Jacquetta was taught to read and write and may have been particularly interested in literature, as attested by the books she owned.

Medieval maidens such as Jacquetta were encouraged to be respectable young ladies and avoid sexual temptations. Christine de Pisan explained that young women should "speak demurely and sweetly" and "must not be frolicsome, forward, or boisterous in speech, expression, bearing or laughter". "This behaviour" Christine further admonished, "would be very unseemly and greatly derisory in a woman of the court in whom there should be more modesty, good manners and courteous behaviour than in any others".[4]

NOTES

[1] Christine de Pizan, *The Treasure of the City of Ladies: Or the Book of the Three Virtues,* ed. Sarah Lawson, p. 3.
[2] BL, Harley MS 4431, ff 1r-177v.
[3] Don S. Browning, Marcia J. Bunge, *Children and Childhood in World Religions: Primary Sources and Texts,* p. 119.
[4] Ibid.

CHAPTER 2:
BECOMING A DUCHESS

As the eldest daughter of the Count of Saint-Pol, Jacquetta was a valuable pawn on the international marriage market. She would have no say in who she would marry for as long as she remained under her family's sphere of influence. When the powerful Duke of Bedford became a widower in November 1432, Jacquetta's uncle Louis, Bishop of Thérouanne, approached him offering Jacquetta as his next bride.

John Plantagenet of Lancaster, first Duke of Bedford, was the third surviving son of King Henry IV of England and Mary de Bohun. Brother of the warrior-king Henry V, he acted as regent of France for his nephew, Henry VI. Henry V died in August 1422, leaving an infant son as his successor. Henry VI was merely nine months old when he became King of England. The Treaty of Troyes of 1420 stipulated that Henry V would marry Catherine of Valois, daughter of the French King Charles VI, and their children would inherit the French crown after Charles's death.

Charles VI's life was blighted with recurring episodes of mental illness that incapacitated him. His fragile health required a regency council, led by the King's wife, Isabeau of Bavaria. Although Charles VI had a son, the dauphin Charles was disinherited and bypassed in favour of sons born to his sister Catherine and Henry V. When Charles VI died in October 1422, Henry VI became the King of France. A regency council was established for the infant king, and Bedford was nominated as regent of France, guarding his royal nephew's inheritance.

How much Jacquetta knew about Bedford prior to their marriage remains unknown, but as regent of France, the duke was a prominent and well-respected figure. He had been regent in Normandy between 1422 and 1432, where the University of Caen was created under his auspices. He enjoyed the reputation of a competent military leader, defeating the French several times, most notably at the Battle of Verneuil. Bedford remained in close contact with Jacquetta's uncle Louis of Luxembourg, Bishop of Thérouanne, who served as Henry VI's chancellor in France.

Bedford's most recent success was the burning of Joan of Arc, a young peasant girl who led Dauphin Charles to his coronation at Reims on 17 July 1429. Joan claimed that she was divinely inspired to bring peace to France by driving out the English from the occupied territories. She claimed that she heard the voices of angels and saints who told her that she would lead the timid dauphin to Reims. Despite Charles's initial hesitation, he was convinced by Joan that she was sent by God and allowed her to lead an army in his name. Her spectacular success over the English at Orléans earned her the sobriquet of "Maid of Orléans" and emboldened Charles to put his trust in her.

Jacquetta may have seen this famous Maid of Orléans during her stay at her uncle's seat at Beaurevoir. In 1430, Joan was captured during the siege of Compiègne and taken to Beaurevoir Castle, the seat of Jacquetta's uncle John of Luxembourg, Count of Ligny. Jacquetta's aunt Jeanne of Béthune and her great-grandmother Jeanne, Dowager Countess of Saint-Pol and Ligny, known as the Demoiselle de Luxembourg, were sympathetic to Joan of Arc. The women supplied her with female clothes, as Joan famously dressed as a man, and interceded on her behalf with the count. Joan later testified that the elderly Countess of Saint-Pol "had requested my lord of Luxembourg that I be not delivered up to the English".[1] It was clear to Jacquetta's womenfolk that if Joan was delivered to the English, she would be executed. When Demoiselle de Luxembourg died on 18 September 1430, Joan of Arc lost a powerful protectress and was soon sold by John of

Luxembourg to the English for ten thousand livres. It was thus Jacquetta's uncle who helped seal Joan of Arc's fate.

In stark contrast to Jacquetta's female kin, Bedford was not sympathetically inclined towards the Maid. To him, she was a raving heretic, "a superstitious and damnable person . . . woman of a disorderly and infamous life, and dissolute manners, dressed in the clothes of a man".[2] When he finally caught her, Bedford could see for himself whether Joan of Arc was who she said she was. She was asked why she was called "the Maid and whether she was one", to which Joan replied defiantly that "I can well say that I am so, and if you do not believe me have me examined by some women". Bedford commissioned his wife, Anne, to oversee the examination of Joan of Arc's virginity, and when Joan was subjected to the physical inspection of respected matrons and midwives, he "stood in a secret place from which he could see Joan examined". When her virginity was confirmed, Bedford's wife forbade the warders who guarded Joan to "offer her any violence", meaning that she bluntly forbade them to rape her.[3]

During her trial, Joan was subjected to a series of long and detailed interrogations by bishops and theologians who wanted to catch her in what they believed were lies.

Yet Joan answered their questions with infuriating precision and dignity, with a whiff of arrogance that they took for the sin of pride. In the end, Joan's trial proved to be a foregone conclusion. She was burned at the stake at Rouen on 30 May 1431, aged about seventeen. Seven months later, on 16 December 1431, Henry VI was crowned as King of France.

Jacquetta's exact thoughts about Joan's mission and execution remain unknown. The prevalent opinion in Europe after Joan's death was that she was a holy woman innocently put to death. If Jacquetta had any sentiments for the maid, she was wise to hide them under a cloak of feigned disapproval. In England, where Jacquetta was soon to move, Joan was strongly condemned as "an enchantress, an organ of the Devil, sent by Satan".[4] The lesson that Jacquetta learned from the tale of how Bedford cruelly handled the case of Joan of Arc was that her future husband was ruthless when it suited him.

On 14 November 1432, Bedford's wife died, aged only twenty-nine. They'd married in 1423, and although they didn't produce any children, they were perceived as a harmonious couple. Bedford's decision to marry Anne in the first place was motivated by politics since she was the sister of the Duke of Burgundy, and Henry V's dying wish was that his brothers should keep peace with him for the sake of his son's inheritance. The cause of Anne's death remains unknown. Chronicler Enguerrand de Monstrelet included a moving description of her death in his work:

"In these days Anne, duchess of Bedford, and sister to the duke of Burgundy, lay ill, at the hotel of the Tournelles in Paris, of a lingering disorder, which in spite of all the care of her physicians, of whom she had many, carried her off from this life. She was buried in the same chapel of the Celestins where Louis, late duke of Orléans, had been interred."[5]

The chronicler asserted that the Duke of Bedford "was sorely afflicted at her death, as were many of his party; for they feared that the connexion, which had been continued by her means with her brother, the duke of Burgundy, would thereby be weakened".[6] Indeed, when Philip the Good learned that his brother-in-law remarried within six months of Anne's death, he was outraged by the breach of trust. Also, Jacquetta's father didn't seek Burgundy's permission as he should have, considering that he was his vassal.

De Monstrelet went on to describe Jacquetta's wedding feast:

"The wedding feasts were celebrated in the episcopal palace of Thérouanne and for the joy and happiness the duke felt in this match (for the damsel was handsome, well made and lively) and that it might be long had in remembrance, he presented to the church of Thérouanne two magnificent bells of great value, which he had sent thither from England at his own cost."[7]

The cathedral was torn down in the 1550s, and so the two magnificent bells that were to commemorate Jacquetta's illustrious marriage no longer toll.

What the seventeen-year-old Jacquetta, new Duchess of Bedford, felt for her much-older husband can only be guessed at. Medieval marriages of prominent political figures were not matters of mutual attraction, but complicated arrangements between powerful dynasties. "The marriage had been long negotiated by the bishop", Jacquetta's prominent uncle, and she was probably never even asked if she wanted to marry. On the other hand, medieval noblewomen were raised to expect the best matches, and Bedford was such a match in terms of rank, influence and financial stability. Jacquetta became a duchess and married into the English royal family, becoming Henry VI's aunt by marriage and outranking her own mother.

If she felt lost and unsure in her new position, Jacquetta could draw consolation from Christine de Pisan's precious advice. It was of paramount importance that a wife should "love her husband and live in peace with him". "The noble princess who would like to follow the rules of honour in all circumstances will behave towards her lord, be he old or young, in all the ways that good faith and true love command", Christine admonished. Jacquetta was supposed to "humble herself towards him in deed and word and by curtsying; she will obey without complaint; and she will hold her peace to the best of her ability".[8]

Jacquetta was now a great lady who had to supervise her husband's large household. In France, the Duke of Bedford owned the Hôtel de Bourbon, a former Parisian town house of the royal family of Bourbon. It was located on the right bank of the river Seine on the rue d'Autriche, between the Louvre Palace to the west and the Church of Saint-Germain l'Auxerrois to the east. The breathtaking great hall, the Grande Salle du Petit-Bourbon, was larger than any room in the Louvre.

In June 1433, Bedford took Jacquetta to England since he had to attend the opening of Parliament. The couple were "worthily received" by the Lord Mayor of London "with all his aldermen and worthy communes of the City".[9] Soon after her arrival to England, Jacquetta requested denization and became an English citizen in the summer of 1433. On 31 August 1433, her father died, and in November a service was held at St Paul's Cathedral in London, which Jacquetta presumably attended.

The duke resided mainly abroad from 1419 to 1435, except for short periods of time he spent in England in 1426-27 and 1433-34. Jacquetta thus lived mainly in English-occupied territories in France, her chief residence being in Rouen.[10] Bedford remodelled the castle in Rouen to fit his needs and expectations and built the manor of Joyeux Repos for his and Jacquetta's private use. In England, Bedford built a manor at Fulbrook in Warwickshire, where he and Jacquetta resided in 1434, when the citizens of Coventry presented the young duchess with fifty marks and a silver-gilt cup.[11] Another grand residence of the Duke and Duchess of Bedford was Penshurst Place in Kent, where the duke made substantial alterations.

In 1434, Jacquetta was made Lady of the Garter to put her on a similar level as her husband's sister-in-law Eleanor Cobham, Duchess of Gloucester, and joined the annual Garter festivities at Windsor Castle on 23 April.[12] Ladies of the Garter supported the male members of the Order of the Garter and wore similar robes and garters, celebrating magnificent ceremonies with their male counterparts. The Order of the Garter was a military order founded by Edward III in 1349 to create a coterie of loyal military men. According to legend, the Order of the Garter was founded in honour of Joan of Kent, Edward III's daughter-in-law. A garter with a French maxim "hony soit qui mal y pense" written on it was worn at the knee to remind the members to behave according to the Order's chivalric code.

In July 1434, the Duke and Duchess of Bedford left for France.[13] The cache of goods, including jewels, plate, liturgical objects, household furnishings as well as books and other portable property that Bedford left behind, was inventoried, providing a window through which we can catch a glimpse of the rich objects Jacquetta was surrounded by on a daily basis.

As regent, Bedford acquired a large collection of jewels and plate, tapestries, books and liturgical textiles from the French royal collection. A great patron and book collector, Bedford obtained the great Louvre royal library of Charles V and Charles VI, of which about one hundred manuscripts still survive today. Jacquetta's copy of Christine de Pisan's *Collected Works*, known as *The Book of the Queen*, was part of this collection. The manuscript was originally assembled for Isabeau of Bavaria, wife and queen of Charles VI. A miniature inside the manuscript shows Christine presenting the book to Isabeau, who is surrounded by her ladies-in-waiting. The likely date of the presentation is New Year's of 1414. Jacquetta treasured this book and inscribed her name inside it; her son Anthony would also own it. When Bedford presented Jacquetta with Christine de Pisan's manuscript remains unknown, but considering Christine's advice for wives and the running of highborn ladies' households, it's likely that the manuscript was a wedding gift.[14]

Another manuscript Jacquetta may have seen in her husband's collection is the *Salisbury Breviary*, currently preserved at the Bibliothèque Nationale de France, ordered by Bedford in the early 1420s. This breviary was originally ordered when the duke was married to Anne of Burgundy, whose images feature prominently throughout the manuscript.[15] Yet the breviary was altered, certainly after Bedford married Jacquetta in 1433, to add the Bedford-Luxembourg coat of arms at the bottom of one of the folios.[16]

Between 1422 and 1433, the duke of Bedford acquired more than two hundred tapestries from the French royal collection, some of which were later added to the English royal collection.[17] Among these tapestries was a series of heraldic hangings incorporating Charles VI's motto "Jamais" as well as a dossal woven with the story of St Clovis; these were later acquired by Henry VI, who featured them prominently in the Presence Chamber at the palace of Westminster.[18]

Bedford's inventory also boasted several beds with matching bedding, curtains and cushions. Beds were highly prized possessions of medieval nobility and were often mentioned as bequests in wills or given as rewards for loyal service. One of Bedford's beds was given to John de Vere, thirteenth Earl of Oxford, in 1485.[19]

A large portion of Bedford's possessions was transferred to the collections of Cardinal Beaufort and Henry VI. Today, only one piece of the Bedford inventories remains: it is the so-called Royal Gold Cup, bejewelled and enamelled with scenes from the life of St Agnes, currently preserved at the British Museum. Its first documented appearance dates from 1391 when John, Duke of Berry, presented it to Charles VI.[20]

Jacquetta's glittering marriage was short-lived as her husband died suddenly on 14 September 1435 during the Congress of Arras at his castle of Joyeux Repos in Rouen. He must have been ailing for some time, as suggested by the presence of the royal physician in the Bedford household. Christine de Pisan, who shaped fifteenth-century women's views, suggested that a good wife "will be very solicitous about her husband's body so that he may be maintained in health and preserved in long life". To achieve this, she "will often want to speak to his physicians and enquire of them about his state of health".[21]

John, Duke of Bedford, was forty-six at the time of his death, and the reason behind his sudden demise remains unknown. He was buried on 30 September at Rouen Cathedral, where he had been received as a canon five years earlier. His black marble monument was mutilated by Calvinists in 1562 during the French Wars of Religion, and the rest of the monument was destroyed in its entirety in the eighteenth century. Bedford's coffin, which remained intact, was opened in October 1866. Scientists examined a lock of the duke's hair and about fifty grams of a blackish substance found inside the coffin; it contained mercurial embalming preservative.[22]

Jacquetta and Bedford had no offspring together, although the duke had two illegitimate children, and Jacquetta would produce a large brood with her second husband. In his last will, the duke made sure that his young wife was well provided for, although he didn't appoint her as one of the executors, an honour he accorded to his first wife, Anne of Burgundy, when he made the first draft of his testament in 1428. This may well have been because of Jacquetta's youth (she was not yet twenty) and not due to any animosity between the spouses.

Jacquetta received twelve thousand livres in goods as well as a life interest in most of Bedford's extensive lands in England, France and Normandy. As a widow, she was entitled to receive a dower, a one-third share of her late husband's lands. She was allowed to start profiting from these lands in England and Calais in 1436 under condition that she wouldn't remarry without royal licence. Although the marriage to John, Duke of Bedford, would define

Jacquetta's status for the years to come, she was not prepared to spend her life in perpetual widowhood.

NOTES

[1] Regine Pernoud, *Joan of Arc: By Herself and Her Witnesses* , p. 156.
[2] Ibid.
[3] Ibid., p. 169.
[4] Edward Hall, *Hall's Chronicle*, p. 568.
[5] J. B. Baron Dacier (ed.), *The Chronicles of Enguerrand de Monstrelet,* p. 100.
[6] Ibid.
[7] Ibid, p. 114.
[8] Christine de Pizan, *The Treasure of the City of Ladies: Or the Book of the Three Virtues*, p. 112.
[9] *Gregory's Chronicle*, pp. 176-177.
[10] Anthony Emery, *Greater Medieval Houses of England and Wales, 1300–1500: Volume 3*, p. 392.
[11] *Coventry Leet Book*, p. 52.
[12] James L. Gillespie, "Ladies of the Fraternity of Saint George and of the Society of the Garter", *Albion: A Quarterly Journal Concerned with British Studies*, Vol. 17, No. 3 (Autumn, 1985), pp. 259-278.
[13] E. Carleton Williams, *My Lord of Bedford 1389-1435*, p. 237.
[14] BL, Harley MS 4431, ff 1r-177v.
[15] The Salisbury Breviary (Paris, Bibliothèque Nationale de France, MS lat. 17294), ff. 283v, 518r.
[16] Ibid., f. 106.
[17] Thomas P. Campbell, Maryan Wynn Ainsworth, *Tapestry in the Renaissance: Art and Magnificence*, p. 17.
[18] Jenny Stratford, *The Bedford Inventories*, p. 89.
[19] Ibid., p. 351.
[20] Ibid., p. 320.
[21] Christine de Pizan, *The Treasure of the City of Ladies*, p. 144.
[22] Philippe Charlier et al. "The Embalming of John of Lancaster, First Duke of Bedford (1435 A. D.): A Forensic Analysis". *Medicine, Science and the Law 56, no. 2 (2016): 107-115.*

Chapter 3:
Marrying for Love

With Bedford's death, Jacquetta became one of the wealthiest young widows in England; the Duke of Bedford's annual income was over £4,000, giving Jacquetta an income of £1,333 per year.[1] Christine de Pisan warned that rich widows were especially vulnerable because "people try to relieve them of their wealth".[2] That was undeniably true in Jacquetta's case as she lost the county of Harcourt to Edmund Beaufort in December 1435. Beautiful and wealthy, Jacquetta was a good catch, and her family wanted to make sure that she chose her next husband wisely. On 28 February 1436, Jacquetta's uncle Louis and Lord Talbot were ordered to make her swear that she would not remarry without the King's licence. Although she agreed, Jacquetta later broke her oath, and by March 1437 she had remarried, proving that she had a will of her own.

The man she chose was Sir Richard Woodville, who served in her late husband's household. The Woodvilles belonged to the minor gentry and held lands in Kent and Northamptonshire. Richard's father served as chamberlain in the household of Jacquetta's first husband and enjoyed the Duke of Bedford's trust and confidence. It was likely through his father's connections that the young Richard Woodville came into Bedford's ducal establishment. No portrait of Richard survives, but he was young and hardworking, and a knight too; he was knighted in 1426. Enguerrand de Monstrelet, a contemporary French chronicler, described him in glowing terms as "a young man, very handsome and well made".

There was no doubt that Jacquetta's second marriage was a love match, but there was also some political calculation to it as well. Richard was her social inferior, and that fact in itself ensured that Jacquetta retained her autonomous position as Duchess of Bedford, a title she never relinquished and used proudly until her death. She would always be her husband's social superior, and Richard would always be castigated as a man who had "made himself by marriage", meaning that he became politically and socially prominent after marrying the Duke of Bedford's widow.[3] Jacquetta's decision to remarry beneath her rank provoked a strong reaction from her relatives. De Monstrelet recorded that:

"In this year, the duchess of Bedford, sister to the count of Saint-Pol, married, out of her own free will, an English knight called Sir Richard Woodville, a young man, very handsome and well made, but, in regard to birth inferior to her first husband, the regent, and to herself. Louis de Luxembourg, archbishop of Rouen, and her other relations, were very angry at this match, but they could not prevent it."[4]

De Monstrelet's assertion that Jacquetta remarried "out of her own free will" is important because it was a common practice in medieval society to kidnap a wealthy heiress in order to marry her and overtake her possessions. Writing in the 1530s, the English chronicler Edward Hall echoed de Monstrelet's sentiment and recorded:

"The Duchess of Bedford, sister to Louis, earl of Saint-Pol, minding also to marry, rather for pleasure than for honour, without counsel of her friends, married a lusty knight called Sir Richard Woodville, to the great displeasure of her uncle the bishop of Thérouanne, and the earl her brother: but they now could not remedy it, for the chance was cast and passed."[5]

Jacquetta's voice can be heard loud and clear across the centuries in a petition to Henry VI, wherein she begged him to pardon her for remarrying without his royal permission. Richard was, in Jacquetta's own words, the King's "true liegeman", and the couple had already suffered "in their persons as in their goods" for their marriage.[6] Her petition was successful, and on 23 March 1437 Jacquetta and Richard were pardoned for "intermarrying without the King's consent", although they were obliged to pay a fine of £1,000 for breaking the royal law.[7]

Jacquetta wasn't the only great lady who remarried without Henry VI's permission. One of the most scandalous examples was the secret marriage of Catherine of Valois, Henry VI's mother, and her Welsh servant, Owen Tudor. Between 1427 and 1428, an act of Parliament forbade dowager queens to remarry without permission of the King or his Privy Council. Two royal widows lived in England at the time, Catherine of Valois and Joan of Navarre (Henry IV's second wife), but the act was aimed specifically at Catherine because at some point in her widowhood it was discovered that she planned to remarry.[8] At first, she was romantically linked with Edmund Beaufort, but their relationship did not last long, and Catherine fell in love with Owen. "The lords of the King's council would not agree to her marrying anyone during the King's minority", the *Giles Chronicle* stated. Anyone who married Catherine was threatened to be "punished in the forfeiture of all goods and in the death penalty as a traitor to the King".[9] Still, Catherine and Owen continued their secret relationship, and the dowager queen gave birth to three children in quick succession.

Jacquetta's choice of a husband had been condemned in the same manner as Catherine of Valois's. Catherine was said to have been "young and lusty, following more her own appetite than friendly counsel, and regarding more her private affection than her open honour".[10] In both cases, it was believed that Jacquetta and Catherine remarried to fulfil their repressed sexual desires. It was a common medieval belief, stemming from ancient Greek philosophers, that marriage could protect women from illnesses that usually afflicted those who abstained from sex. The word "hysteria" appeared first in *On the Diseases of Women* in the Hippocratic Corpus. It was considered a disease of the womb, called "hystera" in Greek. The ancient philosopher Plato explained:

"What is called the matrix or womb, a living creature within them (women) with a desire for child-bearing, if it be left long unfruitful beyond the due season, is vexed and aggrieved, and wandering throughout the body and blocking the channels of the breath, by forbidding respiration brings the sufferer to extreme distress and causes all manner of disorders."[11]

Medieval chroniclers writing about Jacquetta and Catherine's remarriages thus reflected the widespread belief that a woman's judgment was clouded by her sexual urges. It has been recently suggested that Jacquetta may have been pregnant at the time of her clandestine marriage; if true, her pregnancy would have explained why she remarried without royal licence.[12] It is doubtful that Jacquetta served as Catherine of Valois's lady-in-waiting since the dowager queen lived quietly away from court, and by the time Jacquetta remarried she was residing at Bermondsey Abbey, perhaps after her secret marriage had been discovered. Catherine died on 3 January 1437 after what she described as a "long, grievous malady".[13]

Henry VI granted Jacquetta's dower between June and November 1437. On 10 June 1440, Jacquetta and Richard purchased the manor of Grafton in Northamptonshire, their main estate, where they started their family. Children began arriving quickly, and by 1446 Jacquetta was the mother of four boys: Anthony, Richard and two Johns.[14] It is somewhat confusing that two of the Woodville sons were christened John, but it was a common practice among medieval nobility to give the same names to different children in case one of them died young. Jacquetta also had two sons named Richard in honour of her husband.

In July 1441, Richard Woodville accompanied Richard Plantagenet, Duke of York, to Rouen when York was appointed as Lieutenant of France. Jacquetta, listed as "duchess of Bedford", accompanied York's wife, Cecily, with other noblewomen such as "the countess of Oxford, the countess of Ewe, and many other ladies with their lords, and other gentlewomen and damsels that belonged to them".[15] Returning to Rouen was a bittersweet moment for Jacquetta: it was there where her first husband died and was buried in 1435. Also, Jacquetta's uncle Louis, former Bishop of Thérouanne, was the Archbishop of Rouen. The reunion of Jacquetta and Louis couldn't have been a happy family occasion since Louis was much displeased with Jacquetta's marriage to Richard Woodville.

Cecily Neville, Duchess of York, was of similar age to Jacquetta, having been born on 3 May 1415. She was a daughter of Ralph Neville, Earl of Westmorland, and Joan Beaufort. Cecily's mother was one of the four children born to John of Gaunt, Duke of Lancaster, son of King Edward III, and his mistress Katherine Swynford. Gaunt eventually married Katherine and the pope legitimated their children in 1397, but the Beauforts were excluded from royal succession in 1407.

Just like Jacquetta, Cecily was a new mother. Her first child, a daughter named Anne, was born on 11 August 1439. A son, Henry, was born on 10 February 1441 but died in infancy, probably before Cecily moved to Rouen. Having children was a blessing for Cecily because she had been married for ten years before finally becoming pregnant for the first time. As duchesses, Jacquetta and Cecily were the highest-ranking noblewomen in England, and thus it's easy to understand why they started associating in the early 1440s. They had much in common, for besides being of similar age and illustrious parentage, they shared an interest in literature.

Upon Bedford's death, Jacquetta inherited his vast collection of books and manuscripts. The *Salisbury Breviary*, an illustrated office book updated by Bedford during his marriage to Jacquetta, contains Jacquetta's coat of arms: the lion of Luxembourg impaled with Bedford's royal arms.[16] She also owned John Gower's *Confessio Amantis* or *The Lover's Confession.* Jacquetta left her signature and personal motto, "sour tous autres" meaning "above all others", in that manuscript.[17] Jacquetta's motto provides an interesting insight into her personality. The exact origin of the motto remains unknown; it seems likely that the motto implied that Jacquetta felt that as the Duchess of Bedford she stood "above all others" in terms of social rank and education.

Jacquetta also owned a collection containing twenty-nine works by Christine de Pisan. She inscribed her name "Jaquette" and inserted a personal motto in the outer margin of Christine's *Epistre au Dieu d'Amours*.[18] The final book that can be linked to Jacquetta is a collection of travellers' accounts of the East, including *La Fleur des Histoires de la Terre d'Orient*, translated by Jean d'Ypres, and Jean d'Arras's *Roman de Melusine*. Jacquetta's signature was visible on the last folio that was lost in the Cottonian fire of 1731.[19]

Cecily, Duchess of York, also owed *Confessio Amantis* and one of Christine de Pisan's most famous works, *Le Livre de la Cité des Dames* or *The Book of the City of Ladies*. One of the pages includes the badges of the white rose and the fetterlock, linked to the Yorks.[20] Cecily and Jacquetta apparently became close since on 22 September 1444 Jacquetta was chosen as godmother of Cecily's daughter Elizabeth. The baptism took place in the Rouen cathedral where Jacquetta's first husband was buried. The baptism placed Jacquetta in Rouen three years after her departure from England, which means that she had plenty of time to associate with the Duke and Duchess of York. She certainly accompanied Cecily during her confinements and churchings, for the Duchess of York had three children born during her stay at Rouen: Edward, future king, born on 28 April 1442, Edmund, born on 17 May 1443, and the abovementioned Elizabeth, born and baptised on 22 September 1444.

Little did the two young mothers know that their children—Jacquetta's daughter Elizabeth and Cecily's son Edward—would one day marry and sit together on the throne.

NOTES

[1] Michael Hicks, *The Changing Role of the Wydevilles in Yorkist Politics to 1483*, p. 62.
[2] Christine de Pizan, *The Treasure of the City of Ladies*, p. 157.
[3] Sir John Fenn, Alexander Ramsay, *Paston Letters*, p. 105.
[4] Enguerrand de Monstrelet, *La Chronique*, p. 17.
[5] Edward Hall, *Hall's Chronicle*, p. 185.
[6] *Parliament Rolls of Medieval England*, January 1438, item 16.
[7] *CPR, Henry VI, Volume 3, A.D. 1436-1441*, p. 53.
[8] Bertram Wolffe, *Henry VI*, p. 45.
[9] Terry Breverton, *Owen Tudor*, p. 135.
[10] Ibid., p. 138.
[11] James Hillman, *The Myth of Analysis: Three Essays in Archetypal Psychology*, p. 253.
[12] John Ashdown-Hill, *Royal Marriage Secrets*, Kindle edition.
[13] Terry Breverton, *Owen Tudor*, p. 155.
[14] Read more in Appendix 1.
[15] J. L. Laynesmith, *Cecily Duchess of York*, p. 39.
[16] Paris, Bibliothèque Nationale de France, MS lat. 17294, f. 106r.

[17] Cambridge, Pembroke College, MS 307.
[18] BL, Harley MS 4431, ff. 1, 51v, 52v, 115v.
[19] BL, Cotton MS Otho D II.
[20] BL, Royal MS 19 A XIX.

Chapter 4:
Coming of the Queen

Jacquetta knew that at some point in his life Henry VI would have to marry and settle the succession. Henry's court was a male preserve, and it had been a long time since the country had a Queen consort. The King's mother, Catherine of Valois, died on 3 January 1437, leaving three children behind. Another royal woman, Henry's step-grandmother, Joan of Navarre (second wife of Henry IV), died on 10 June 1437. The King's English aunts were either dead (Margaret, Duchess of Clarence, died in 1439) or in disgrace (Eleanor, Duchess of Gloucester, was sentenced to perpetual imprisonment after she was found guilty of witchcraft in 1441). Despite her remarriage, Jacquetta Woodville was the closest female relative of Henry VI. She was his aunt by marriage, although she was only four years older than the King.

By the time Henry VI turned twenty, he needed a wife and an heir to further his dynasty. Despite the later tales of the saintly King cringing at the sight of dancing ladies with low-cut décolletages, he wanted to make sure that a woman with whom he was to share every private moment was as good-looking as she was pious. True, he was unusually virtuous for a king, as noticed by Italian humanist Piero da Monte, who wrote that at the age of sixteen, Henry VI "avoided the sight and conversation of women, affirming these to be the work of the devil". Like most of his male contemporaries, Henry VI perceived women as sexual beings who often lured men into sin. The King's confessor, John Blacman, asserted that Henry "made a covenant with his eyes that they should never look unchastely upon any woman". This was in keeping with Jesus's teachings: "But I say unto you, that whosoever looked on a woman to lust after her hath committed adultery with her already in his heart" (Matthew 5: 27-28). "Those who knew him intimately said that he had preserved his virginity of mind and body to this present time", da Monte wrote, adding that Henry VI "was firmly resolved to have intercourse with no woman unless within the bounds of matrimony".[1]

In 1442, when negotiations for a marriage with one of the daughters of the Count of Armagnac were set in motion, Henry sent instructions for his ambassadors. These instructions, signed in the King's own hand, carried highly personal requests. The ambassadors were to obtain portraits of the young women "in their kirtles simple, and their faces, like as you see their stature and their beauty and colour of skin and their countenances, with all manner of features".[2]

In the end, the King did not marry one of the daughters of the Count of Armagnac. His choice fell upon Margaret, the daughter of René of Anjou, titular King of Naples, Jerusalem and Sicily as well as Duke of Anjou. Many English people believed that the marriage was not a prestigious match for Henry VI. Margaret of Anjou was merely the King of France's niece by marriage—her paternal aunt, Mary of Anjou, was his spouse—and Charles VII was unwilling to sacrifice one of his daughters for the sake of an English alliance. The future Queen of England came to her new country virtually dowerless, but it was hoped that the marriage would at least bring peace and an end to the Hundred Years' War. The couple married by proxy on 24 May 1444. By early 1445, the young Queen was on her way to England.

In November 1444, Jacquetta set sail for France on board a ship called the *Swallow* while Richard travelled in a smaller boat. In many respects, Jacquetta was the most suitable candidate to welcome the Queen. She was formerly the first lady in English-occupied territories in France, and despite her remarriage she still used the title of Duchess of

Bedford. They were both Frenchwomen who took up residence in England and were linked by ties of kinship: Jacquetta's younger sister Isabel had recently married Charles of Anjou, Margaret's uncle.

On 18 March 1445, Margaret reached Pontoise in northern France, where she was greeted by Richard, Duke of York, who escorted the Queen to Rouen, Normandy's bustling capital. Henry VI sent a richly bedecked chariot to carry Margaret through the city, but his bride was so unwell after the voyage that she was replaced during the procession by William de la Pole's wife, Alice Chaucer.

In Rouen, Margaret, still indisposed, met the English noblewomen, with Jacquetta, Duchess of Bedford, and Cecily, Duchess of York, the most prominent among them. The Queen's attention was caught by the luxurious clothes worn by her new subjects. Chronicler Matthew d'Escouchy noted that they were "most highly and richly dressed".[3] Cecily had many ensembles, one of them costing the staggering amount of £215. One of her dresses was minutely described in wardrobe accounts: it was a surcoat (sleeveless outer gown), mantle and headpiece made of crimson velvet with ermine fur and at least two hundred pearls sewn into the costly materials.[4]

Jacquetta probably wore something similarly opulent, but description of her gowns for Margaret of Anjou's arrival is sadly lost. Still, we can reconstruct what she wore based on the fashion in vogue in fifteenth-century France and England. A miniature of Margaret of Anjou accompanied by two ladies-in-waiting in the *Talbot Shrewsbury Book*, dating to 1445, may represent Jacquetta and Cecily since they were the highest-ranking noblewomen in the Queen's household.[5]

The *Talbot Shrewsbury Book* is a collection of fifteen romances, chivalric treatises, instructional texts, chronicles and statutes compiled as a gift to Margaret of Anjou on the occasion of her betrothal to Henry VI, from John Talbot, first Earl of Shrewsbury, who was among the nobles escorting her to England for her marriage. The noblewomen behind the Queen wear gowns in blue and yellow with low-cut décolletages and furred sleeves. Their gowns, called houppelandes, are clasped with a wide belt just beneath their bosoms to accentuate their slender figures. On their heads, they wear double-lobed headdresses in the shape of a heart, decorated with precious stones and jewels.

Another page in the *Talbot Shrewsbury Book* shows an illustration of noblewomen and men engaged in a discussion about the values of chivalry.[6] Women wear gowns made of copious materials in various colours. Their long sleeves are either short or reaching to the floor, with various types of furs lining them.

The fifteenth century was a time when noblewomen became very extravagant in their outfits. Christine de Pisan warned against "extravagant headdresses and gowns that some women wear", linking them with pride and foolishness.[7] French poet Jean Juvénal des Ursins was outraged by the revealing clothes worn by the ladies-in-waiting at Charles VII's court, and in 1445 he wrote to his brother that the King should "prohibit openings in front through which you can see the women's nipples and breasts, and the great furred trains, girdles and other things, because they are so displeasing to God and the world, and not without reason".[8]

Headdresses or "hennins", as they were known back then, were viciously denounced by clerics and moralists. "Hennin" was a catch-all phrase for various types of headgear worn by women. In the 1440s and 1450s, the most fashionable were horned headdresses that were either very wide or very high, depending on the wearer's inclination. Des Ursins wrote that many women "lived in great and excessive states with marvellous horns, long and large . . . having on each side two great wings so huge that when they wished to pass through doorways they needed to turn sideways and crouch or they would be unable to pass through".[9]

French and English fashions were also heavily influenced by Burgundian trends. Roger van der Weyden's portrait of Isabella of Portugal, Duchess of Burgundy, painted c. 1440, shows what kind of materials a rich noblewoman wore. She wears a horned headdress with pendent veils of lawn. Her dress is made of red cloth of gold edged with ermine and is clasped with a wide green belt beneath her breasts.

From Rouen, Margaret travelled to Harfleur, where she embarked on a ship called the *Cock John* and landed in Portchester on 9 April 1445. It was a dangerous crossing, with the high waves pounding and tossing the ship like a toy. Soon after her arrival, the Queen was sick at Southampton. Henry VI wrote that "our most dear and best beloved wife the Queen is yet sick of the labour and indisposition of the sea, by occasion of which the pox had been broken out upon her". "Master Francisco, the Queen's physician" was paid for various "aromatic confections, particularly and specially purchased by him, and privately made into medicine for the preservation of the health of the said lady".[10] The exact nature of Margaret's illness is not known, but she was well enough for Margaret Chamberlain, the dressmaker who made Cecily Neville's clothes, to visit the Queen at Southampton and take measurements for a new gown.

If one Italian contemporary, Raffaelo de Negra, writing in 1458, is to be believed, Margaret received another visitor, much more important than a physician or a dressmaker. In a letter to his royal mistress, Bianca Maria Visconti, Duchess of Milan, de Negra included a story relayed to him by an Englishman who told him what occurred upon Margaret's landing in England. Henry VI was very eager to meet his bride in person, but he wanted first to observe her from a distance. He decided to dress up as a squire and deliver a letter from the King to Margret.

"While the Queen read the letter the King took stock of [observed] her, saying that a woman may be seen very well when she reads a letter, and the Queen never found out it was the King because she was so engrossed in reading the letter, and she never looked at the King in his squire's dress, who remained on his knees all the time". It was only after the squire left that his true identity was revealed to Margaret, who was "vexed" that she did not recognise him and had kept him on his knees. Raffaelo de Negra, who saw Margaret, described her as "a most handsome woman, though somewhat dark", but whether he was referring to her complexion or hair colour remains unknown.[11]

Margaret was generally reputed to have been beautiful. Georges Chastellain, Burgundian chronicler and poet, called her the exemplification of "all that is majestic in woman" and one of the "most beautiful" persons in the world. "She was indeed a very fair lady, altogether well worth the looking at, and of high bearing withal", he enthused.[12] Chronicler Edward Hall, writing in the mid-sixteenth century, asserted that "this woman excelled all others, as well in beauty and favour, as in wit and policy".[13]

There are several contemporary depictions of Margaret in manuscripts, although some of them may be generic. The most famous of all is the miniature in the *Talbot Shrewsbury Book* dating to 1445. Inside, there is a scene of the manuscript being presented to Margaret of Anjou by the kneeling John Talbot. Margaret is shown enthroned with Henry and crowned as the Queen of England, wearing a purple cloak furred with ermine and fastened with a golden button at the neck. Her long blond hair cascades in loose waves down her back.[14]

Another contemporary image is the prayer roll of Margaret of Anjou, which belongs to the Jesus College at Oxford. It shows Margaret kneeling piously at her prie-dieu, fingertips touching in prayer. Again, she is crowned and wears a purple cloak with a blue gown showing beneath it, and her auburn hair hangs loosely down her back.[15]

There is also a stained-glass window in the church of the Cordeliers at Angers showing Margaret kneeling in prayer, but this is an eighteenth-century copy of a fifteenth-century original. There is also a medal struck by Pietro da Milano c. 1463 when Margaret was in her early thirties. It depicts her posing in profile, with a prominently long nose, heavy-lidded eyes and a swan-like neck.

Henry VI married Margaret of Anjou on 22 April 1445 in Titchfield Abbey. Margaret's wedding jewellery was prepared in January; she received a "ring of gold, garnished with a fair ruby".[16] Henry VI had the ring he received during his coronation as King of France in Paris remade for Margaret. The ring was so valuable that it was kept in the royal collection during Henry VIII's reign; in 1530, it was recorded that a silver-gilt box contained "the ring wherewith Henry VI espoused his Queen".[17]

The description of the wedding ceremony itself is lost to the sands of time, but Margaret's coronation is well documented. A series of elaborately staged pageants designed for the Queen's London reception encapsulated hopes for the future. Margaret was hailed as the bringer of peace with France and the mother of prospective heirs to the throne. London Bridge featured the first pageant where the figures of Plenty and Peace greeted Margaret, presenting her with a biblical injunction to be fruitful and multiply. The second pageant displayed upon the bridge compared Margaret to the dove that brought a "branch of peace" to the biblical Noah, who was saved from the Great Flood.[18]

The Queen rode to Westminster Abbey in a litter bedecked with white cloth of gold, wearing a cornet of "gold, rich pearls and precious stones" upon her head. The magnificence of her jewels can be glimpsed from a letter Henry VI penned to his treasurer shortly before the coronation. The King ordered "such things as our right entirely well-beloved wife the Queen must necessarily have for the solemnity of her coronation". These included a decorative collar garnished with pearls, rubies and sapphires; a golden pectoral garnished with rubies, pearls and diamonds and a brooch that cost two thousand marks.[19]

After the splendid ceremony, there was only one duty the Queen was expected to perform and that was becoming pregnant as soon as possible.

NOTES

[1] Pierro da Monte, as cited in K. Dockray (ed), *A Source Book*, p. 4.

[2] A.R. Myers, *English Historical Documents*, Volume IV, p. 252.

[3] J.L. Laynesmith, *Cecily Duchess of York*, p. 47.

[4] Ibid.

[5] BL, Royal MS 15 E VI, f. 2v.

[6] Ibid., f. 403r.

[7] Christine de Pisan, *The Treasure of the City of Ladies*,p. 117.

[8] M.G.A. Vale, *Charles VII*, p. 94.

[9] Laura Delbrugge, *Self-Fashioning and Assumptions of Identity in Medieval and Early Modern Iberia*, p. 69.

[10] Mary Ann Hookham, *The Life and Times of Margaret of Anjou*, Volume 1, p. 267.

[11] *Calendar of State Papers and Manuscripts in the Archives and Collections of Milan 1385-1618*, n. 26.

[12] Agnes Strickland, *Lives of the Queens of England*, Volume 2, p. 283.

[13] Edward Hall, *Hall's Chronicle*, pp. 204-205.

[14] Chris Green, *The Talbot Shrewsbury Book Goes Online*, http://blogs.bl.uk/digitisedmanuscripts/2012/07/the-talbot-shrewsbury-book-goes-online.html

[15] Bodleian Library, Jesus MS 124. Christopher Muttukumaru, The prayer roll of Margaret of Anjou, she wolf of France https://jesuslibraries.wordpress.com/2017/09/05/the-prayer-roll-of-margaret-of-anjou-she-wolf-of-france/

[16] Foedera V, I, p. 139.

[17] *Letters and Papers, Foreign and Domestic, Henry VIII*, Volume 4, n. 6789.

[18] Helen E. Maurer, *Margaret of Anjou, Queenship and Power in Late Medieval England*, p. 20.

---

[19] Mary Ann Hookham, *The Life and Times of Margaret of Anjou,* Volume 1, pp. 418-419.

CHAPTER 5:
SERVING THE MAD KING

Margaret of Anjou's arrival changed Jacquetta Woodville's life significantly because now she had a royal mistress to serve and could pursue a career as a lady-in-waiting. In addition to the income from her numerous lands and estates, she also drew a salary as the Queen's servant. Jacquetta and her husband were highly favoured by the royal couple, as evidenced by numerous grants and gifts they received over the years. On 9 May 1448, Richard Woodville was created Baron Rivers. Jacquetta was entitled to be styled as Lady Rivers, but she always adhered to her superior title of Duchess of Bedford. Richard continued in the royal service and became one of the King's most favoured men. In December 1448, he received from the King the manor of West Thurrock in Essex in recognition of his "good service in the wars in France and Normandy".[1] In June 1450, he helped quash Jack Cade's rebellion and was admitted to the Order of the Garter in August that same year.

Margaret of Anjou's surviving jewel accounts for the years 1445-49 and 1451-53 show that Jacquetta and her servants were recipients of numerous gifts. In 1447, she received a silver cup worth £35, and in 1452 she was presented with a golden tablet adorned with sapphires costing £16. Jacquetta's presents were among the highest-valued gifts. Other women who received equally expensive objects from the Queen were Anne Stafford, Duchess of Buckingham, and Eleanor Beauchamp, Duchess of Somerset.[2]

Serving the King and Queen was becoming ever-more dangerous as Margaret of Anjou was becoming increasingly unpopular. The people of England blamed her for the losses of the hard-won French territories, mainly Anjou and Maine, the ancestral inheritance of the Plantagenet dynasty. Such sentiments were not entirely baseless, as correspondence between the Queen and her ally, Charles VII of France, attests. It's clear that Margaret used her influence with the King on behalf of her father and uncle to secure the surrender of Maine and Anjou. In one letter, Henry VI referred to Margaret as "our most dear and well-beloved companion the queen" who "requested us to do this many times".[3]

The loss of Normandy in particular in 1449 created widespread discontent and crisis in Henry VI's government. In the power struggles of the court, Margaret allied herself first with William de la Pole, Duke of Suffolk, and then with Edmund Beaufort, second Duke of Somerset. William de la Pole bore the brunt of criticism for the disasters in France, especially because he was perceived as the architect of the King's marriage with Margaret and the Queen was seen as the power behind the throne. Suffolk was impeached in January 1450 during the second session of the Parliament that began in the autumn of 1449, and many demanded his head. Yet Henry VI and Margaret of Anjou decided to protect their favourite, and the King merely banished Suffolk from England for a period of five years.

Today, many historians repeat the myth that Margaret of Anjou and William de la Pole were lovers. This claim was first put forward in the sixteenth century by chronicler Edward Hall, who stated that Suffolk was "the Queen's darling".[4] It was William Shakespeare in the late sixteenth century who wrote a love affair between the two into his play about Henry VI's reign. There's no contemporary source naming Suffolk as Margaret's paramour. She favoured him and his wife, Alice, and, considering the age gap between them, it's likely that the Queen considered Suffolk more like a father than a romantic figure.

The King's decision proved highly unpopular, and many speculated that he would lose his crown for it.[5] Yet Suffolk didn't leave the shores of England alive; his ship was intercepted, and the duke was beheaded with a rusty sword after a mock-trial on board ship. His body was left on the beach at Dover, with his head stuck on a pole beside it. Suffolk's death was not the end of the hatred directed towards him, however. Alice de la Pole, now Dowager Duchess of Suffolk, was perceived as one of the Queen's closest companions, and, as the widow of a traitor, she was an object of derision and mockery. During the session of Parliament in November 1450, the Commons sought to try her for treason and demanded her removal from court. They also tried to attaint Suffolk, which would result in Alice losing her dower.

Although she was also a close friend and lady-in-waiting of the Queen's, Jacquetta was not named among the influential persons in 1450. This may be because her frequent pregnancies kept her away from court. Jacquetta certainly rejoiced when, in early 1453, Queen Margaret discovered she was pregnant as well. Bearing children was the essential task of medieval consorts, and the Queen was well aware that she was expected to deliver a male heir. By 1453, Jacquetta herself was the mother of at least eleven children. Her eldest daughter, Elizabeth, was now about sixteen years old, and it was time for Jacquetta and Richard to plan for her future. Writing in the sixteenth century, Sir Thomas More asserted that Elizabeth Woodville "was in service with Queen Margaret" either as maid of honour or lady-in-waiting, but this notion has been dismissed by Elizabeth's modern biographers.[6] There was an "Elizabeth Grey" in Queen Margaret's household, but she may have been Isabella Grey (who was much older than Jacquetta's daughter), or Elizabeth, the widow of Ralph Grey of Heaton, who was serving the Queen in 1445.[7]

In 1842's *History and Antiquities of Charnwood Forest*, T.R. Potter quoted from the document entitled "Elizabeth Wydeville's Diary", which was then reported to be a genuine daily account written by the young Elizabeth while she was living with her parents in their manor at Grafton. The diary had been dismissed by several scholars as a forgery or likely to have been part of a novel written by Elizabeth Benger in the nineteenth century. Historian David Baldwin defended its authenticity, arguing that "it's not an obvious forgery written by someone who plainly had little or no knowledge of life at the end of the Middle Ages".[8] One entry in particular convinced Baldwin that the diary may be authentic, and it's an entry where Elizabeth mentions her mother, Jacquetta:

"Seven o'clock—went out with the Lady Duchess, my mother, into the court-yard, fed five and thirty men and women; chid Roger very severely for expressing some dissatisfaction in attending us with the broken meat."[9]

Baldwin stated that it's likely that the Woodvilles "displayed their largesse by feeding a number of poor people with the surplus left over from their own meals". The original manuscript, that was said to have been "locked up in Drummond Castle" in Lincolnshire, cannot be currently located, and its existence was never confirmed.[10]

At some point in the early 1450s, Elizabeth Woodville married John Grey, son of Sir Edward Grey and Elizabeth Ferrers, who held the title of Baroness Ferrers of Groby in her own right. It was a good match, but not as illustrious as the match the Duchess of York managed to secure for her eldest daughter. Anne of York was born in 1439, so she was similar in age to Elizabeth Woodville. She married in January 1446 at the age of six. Her groom was Henry Holland, then fifteen years old, heir to John Holland, second Duke of Exeter. It was a prestigious match that would make Anne of York a duchess upon her father-in-law's death and one that linked her to royalty since Henry Holland was a descendant of John of Gaunt, Duke of Lancaster. The little Anne Holland became a duchess quicker than anyone anticipated since her husband's father died in July 1447. Jacquetta's eldest daughter didn't marry an earl's or a duke's heir, but she would one day marry a king. For the time being, she busied herself with bearing John Grey's children. Jacquetta's first grandchild, Thomas, was born shortly after the marriage, probably between 1451 and 1455. Jacquetta was then in her mid-thirties and still pregnant on an almost annual basis herself.

Many people in England, Jacquetta certainly among them, wondered why it took the royal couple eight years to beget a child. Henry VI was said to make the decision of abstaining from sexual intercourse with his wife early in their marriage. In October 1446, one year into the marriage, it was rumoured that Bishop Aiscough of Salisbury, the Earl of Suffolk and others kept the King from "having his sport" with the Queen.[11] This may well have been true since Margaret was only sixteen at the time, and contemporaries believed that early childbearing could be mortally dangerous for women. Also, Henry VI was very pious and may have insisted on not having sex with Margaret when sexual activity was prohibited by the Church. Sundays, Lent and saint's days were debarred, although many people indulged in intimate relations nevertheless. It is equally possible that Margaret was pregnant before 1453 but had miscarriages that were not recorded.

In any case, she understood that a failure to provide a male heir cast a shadow of doubt on her fertility and blighted her queenship. Soon after her marriage, rumours circulated in England that she was barren. In 1448, a prisoner in Canterbury gaol accused his neighbour of saying that "our queen was not able to be Queen of England . . . because she bore no child and because we have no prince in this land".[12] Three years later Thomas Young, councillor to Richard Plantagenet, Duke of York, complained of the Queen's inability to produce children and proposed in Parliament that York should be recognised as the King's heir presumptive.

Margaret was humiliated, but she didn't lose hope. If it was any consolation for her, the King never took a mistress because he "eschewed all licentiousness in word or deed" and "with her and towards her he kept his marriage vow wholly and sincerely even in the absences of the lady, which were sometimes very long". Margaret was most likely Henry's only sexual partner, as he was "chaste and pure from the beginning of his days" until his marriage to Margaret.[13]

Jacquetta's initial reaction to Margaret's pregnancy was not recorded, but it may have been similar to what Cecily, Duchess of York, felt when she wrote a congratulatory letter to the Queen. Cecily described the child in Margaret's belly as "the most precious, most joyful, and most comfortable earthly treasure that might come unto this land and to the people thereof".[14] The birth of a son would effectively put an end to uncertainty over the succession and cement Margaret of Anjou's position as Queen.

Everyone's happiness soon turned to desperation, however. In August 1453, during the third trimester of Margaret of Anjou's pregnancy, the King suffered a complete mental breakdown that left him unresponsive for a year and a half. Throughout his life, Henry VI was considered mentally simple. His intimate friend and admirer, John Blacman, once said that the King was "a simple man, without craftiness or untruth, as is plain to all". "Simple" in this context meant that Henry was honest and devoid of the guile that characterised so many of his contemporaries. "With none did he deal craftily, nor ever would say an untrue word", Blackman later recorded in his biography of the King.[15] Yet there are hints that Henry was mentally unstable prior to the complete breakdown he suffered in 1453.

In 1440, allegations emerged that Eleanor Cobham, Duchess of Gloucester, had enlisted two men who had used astrology and necromancy to predict the death of Henry VI. According to their horoscope, the King would die of melancholy at the age of twenty. "Melancholy" was a common term for depression during the Middle Ages, so perhaps Henry showed symptoms of his mental illness as early as 1440. In 1450, it was rumoured that "the King was a natural fool and would often hold a staff in his hands with a bird on the end, playing therewith as a fool, and that another king must be ordained to rule the land, saying that the king was no person able to rule the land".[16] It was also suggested that Henry had a childlike face and was "not steadfast of wit as other kings have been before". In 1453, prior to Henry's breakdown, he was said to have been "but a sheep" who has "lost all that his father won and would God he had died soon after he was born".[17] General perception of the King as a meek, mild-mannered and modest man contributed to more rumours about the state of his mental health.

The diagnosis of the illness that removed the King from the political scene for eighteen months is shrouded in mystery; historians today describe his state as catatonic, suspecting that he suffered from schizophrenia. Mental illness had been passed down for several generations in Henry VI's line. His great-grandmother, Joanna of Bourbon, suffered a severe mental collapse after she gave birth to her seventh child, although her already fragile mental condition may have been triggered by childbirth, plunging her into postpartum depression or psychosis. Contemporaries recorded only that she "lost her good sense and her good memory" but recovered within months; her condition must have been serious since her husband, Charles V, went on a pilgrimage and offered many prayers for her recovery.[18] She eventually recovered but died five years later, in 1378, after giving birth to her ninth child. Chronicler Froissart ascribed the cause of Jeanne's death to her fervent wish to take a bath in the days following her daughter Catherine's birth. The wording of Froissart's chronicle suggests that Jeanne suffered from another mental breakdown since "the queen being in childbed, was not well at ease, and her physicians had cautioned her that she should on no account enter into any bath, for they said it was contrary to her disease, and very dangerous for her".[19]

Jeanne's eldest son, Charles VI, suffered from mental illness as well. He experienced hallucinations, delusions and at one point believed he was made of glass, forbidding anyone to come near him for fear he would shatter into pieces. He also believed that he was bewitched, as mental illness was not understood then as it is now.

Abbot Wethamsted, who saw Henry VI at some point between the onset of his malady and his recovery, reported that:

"A disease and disorder of some sort overcame the King [in 1453] that he completely lost his wits and memory for a time, and nearly all his body was so uncoordinated and out of control that he could neither walk, nor hold his head upright, nor easily move from where he sat."[20]

At first, the King's physicians decided to wait and see how Henry's condition would develop; they hoped that his illness would disappear as unexpectedly as it had appeared. Many hoped that the birth of his son would rouse Henry from his stupor, and while the King had been carefully attended by his physicians, the Queen was preparing for the arrival of their first child.

In England, it was customary for women to withdraw from public life about a month before their approaching delivery, and Margaret established her birthing chamber at Windsor Castle. Men were not allowed to invade this all-female sanctum. Instead of the usually appointed male officers, ladies-in-waiting were to temporarily perform their tasks. They were to serve as "butlers, pantlers (keepers of the pantry), sewers, carvers, cup bearers; and all manner of officers shall bring to them all manner of things to the great chamber door".[21] The Queen gave birth on 13 October 1453. The child was named Edward since he was born on the feast of the translation of Edward the Confessor. The next day Edward was baptised at Westminster Abbey. His godparents were Cardinal Kempt; Edmund Beaufort, Duke of Somerset; and Anne Stafford, Duchess of Buckingham, the sister of Cecily Neville.

The Queen's churching, her re-entrance into the public life, was scheduled to take place on 18 November. Thirty-five noblewomen received invitations to take part in the ceremony, and chief amongst them were Jacquetta Woodville, Duchess of Bedford, and Cecily Neville, Duchess of York. Jacquetta, heading the list, was still the highest-ranking noblewoman after the Queen, her social status unaffected by her remarriage.[22]

During the ceremony of postbaptismal purification, the Queen left her bedchamber and headed the solemn procession to the church, wherein she heard Mass and offered at the altar. The ceremony started in the Queen's bedchamber, where she awaited the arrival of the nobles in her bed of estate, with the curtains drawn. When nobles came in, two of the highest-ranking duchesses—Jacquetta and Cecily—solemnly drew back the bed curtains, and two noblemen then lifted the Queen to her feet. The whole procession would then pass towards the chapel, where the Queen was blessed and sprinkled with holy water.

It soon became apparent that Henry VI would continue in his stupor. In early 1454, Margaret of Anjou decided to seek regency during her husband's instability and submitted "a bill of five articles the first of which is that she desires the whole rule of this land". The idea of a woman wielding absolute power was unheard of in England, and although the Queen's articles were not rejected outright, the leading noblemen were outraged that Margaret aspired to have such power over them. In France, Margaret's homeland, women were often appointed as regents for their absent husbands or underage sons. Margaret's own mother, Isabella of Lorraine, and her grandmother, Yolanda of Aragon, were regents during the minority of their sons. In England, however, women were rarely appointed regents. Still fresh in collective memory was the example of Isabella of France, who rebelled against Edward II and became regent for her son Edward III between 1327 and 1330. It was a period of disaster and incompetence, and no one wanted another Frenchwoman at the head of the government.

Before she could become regent, Margaret of Anjou had to make sure that the King acknowledged their child as his. Rumours had already been circulating that the prince may not have been a royal child at all, but a changeling. Desperate to prove malicious rumours wrong, in January 1454 the Queen arranged for the baby to be brought to Henry VI's presence so that he could bless him. At first, it was Humphrey Stafford, Duke of Buckingham, who took Prince Edward into his arms "and presented him to the King in goodly fashion, beseeching the King to bless him; but the King gave no answer". Then Margaret "came in, took the prince in her arms and presented him as the duke had done, desiring the King to bless him: however, all their labour were in vain, for they departed thence without any answer or expression from the King, saving only that he once looked on the prince and cast his eyes down again, without any more [sign of recognition]".[23] Margaret's bid for the regency also proved unsuccessful, and in March 1454 it was Richard, Duke of York, who became regent after Prince Edward was accepted as heir to the throne by Parliament.

In March 1454, three new physicians and two surgeons were appointed to attend upon Henry VI. They applied a host of remedies known in medieval medicine, hoping to cure the King of his catatonic stupor. They applied potions, waters, laxatives, head-purges, gargles, blood-letting and incisions, among others. Nothing helped, but on Christmas Day 1454 Henry VI came out of his stupor as abruptly as he had fallen into it. He had no recollection of the past eighteen months, and when he learned that he now had a son and heir, he "commanded his almoner to ride to Canterbury with his offering and commanded the secretary to offer at St Edward's". On 9 January 1455, Margaret of Anjou decided to act and gathered the court to witness the meeting between Henry VI and his son. When the King asked his wife what name she had chosen for their child, she replied his name was Edward, and then Henry "held up his hands and thanked God thereof".[24] With this gesture, he acknowledged Prince Edward as his son and heir.

Henry VI's recovery marked the end of Richard of York's protectorate. Almost immediately upon his recovery, the King ordered the release of Edmund Beaufort, second Duke of Somerset, York's enemy, from the Tower. After William de la Pole's death, Somerset had become one of the Queen's chief advisors. He too is often said to have been Margaret's lover, although there's no evidence of an improper relationship between them in primary sources.

Angered by the rise of his political rival, Somerset, and his own exclusion from politics, Richard of York could no longer tolerate the political situation in England and allied himself with his wife's kinsmen, the Earls of Salisbury and Warwick. Richard Neville, fifth Earl of Salisbury, was the elder brother of Cecily, Duchess of York, and his son, also named Richard Neville, was the sixteenth Earl of Warwick and thus Cecily's nephew.

Determined to depose Somerset, York's army attacked the King and his cavalcade on their way to Parliament at Leicester. On 22 May 1455, the first battle in the Wars of the Roses was fought at St Albans, and "many perished on both sides". Somerset was captured and summarily executed. The Milanese ambassador reported that:

"With his death the battle ceased at once and, without loss of time, the Duke of York went to kneel before the King and ask pardon for himself and his followers, as they had not done this in order to inflict any hurt upon his Majesty, but in order to have Somerset. Accordingly the King pardoned them, and on the 23rd the King and York and all returned to London. On the 24th they made the solemn procession, and now peace reigns. The King has forbidden any one to speak about it upon pain of death. The Duke of York has the government, and the people are very pleased at this."[25]

Jacquetta Woodville's husband didn't participate in the battle because he was residing in Calais from September 1451 to August 1455. Richard was recalled to England shortly after York's victory and reunited with Jacquetta and their children. In October 1455, rumours circulated in England that Henry VI had relapsed into his catatonic stupor. "So much rumour is here", wrote one James Gresham to John Paston, adding that "some men fear he is sick again".[26] In November, York's second protectorate was established, to the Queen's chagrin. This time, however, Henry quickly recovered, and in early 1456 York's second protectorate came to an end.

Margaret of Anjou decided to leave London for Tutbury Castle, where she felt safer, and urged the King to establish their powerbase outside London. The Queen was becoming an increasingly unpopular figure, and slurs started being cast at the prince by the Duke of York's followers. Henry and Margaret ruthlessly dealt with such rumours. On 23 February 1456, one John Helton, an apprentice at Gray's Inn, was executed for creating bills claiming that Prince Edward was not the Queen's son. The rumour suggested that Margaret was barren and faked her pregnancy or that she covered up a stillbirth by substituting her child with a changeling.[27] The rumours would continue, prompting a declaration from a contemporary chronicler: "The Queen was defamed and slandered that he that was called Prince was not her son but a bastard gotten in adultery". The royal couple was alarmed by such slanders and in March 1457 ordered the London Common Council to warn "the City companies not to meddle in affairs touching the King, Queen or Prince, but to curb their tongues and not utter any unseemly, scandalous or disgraceful words at their peril".[28]

Jacquetta Woodville was by the Queen's side when these rumours first broke out. She had assisted Margaret in the birthing chamber and attended the Queen's churching ceremony, and she knew for certain that Prince Edward was not a changeling. She and her husband loyally served Henry and Margaret and followed the royal household when it moved to Midlands in the spring of 1456. During her stay in the Midlands, the Queen often visited Coventry, the town staunchly loyal to her. On 14 September 1456, a series of elaborately staged pageants greeted Margaret when she entered Coventry with her retinue. Among the lavishly dressed figures reciting their carefully rehearsed speeches were Isaiah and Jeremiah, Edward the Confessor and John the Evangelist, the four cardinal virtues of Righteousness, Temperance, Strength, and Prudence, and the nine worthies—Hector, Alexander, Joshua, David, Judas Maccabaeus, Arthur, Charlemagne, Caesar and Godfrey of Bouillon. As if in tribute to the Queen's courage, her namesake, St Margaret, was depicted slaying a dragon.

Jacquetta and her husband, Richard, were with the Queen on that occasion. Honouring Lord Rivers as one of the most important men in the Queen's retinue, the Lord Mayor of Coventry presented him with a glass of rosewater.[29] The Woodvilles may have well shared the opinion of one of the Paston correspondents who, in February 1456, described Margaret as "a great and strong laboured woman who spared no pain to sue her things to an intent and conclusion to her power".[30] A year later, in June 1457, Jacquetta and Richard witnessed as Margaret and Henry made their grand entrance to Coventry on

Whitsunday, both wearing their crowns. Jacquetta was among the many "ladies in their mantles, surcoats and other apparel to their estates accustomed" who followed after the Queen and the Duchess of Buckingham, who carried her train on that occasion.[31]

In early 1458, the Great Council met at Westminster to discuss the rebellion of Richard, Duke of York. Although the King was absent, he supported that the council "strove for peace between the lords". On 25 March, the King organised a solemn procession at St Paul's Cathedral celebrating "concord and unity" between the royal family and warring lords. During the "Loveday" procession, the Queen went into the cathedral hand in hand with Richard of York. In the following weeks, a great joust was held at Greenwich. Jacquetta's eldest son, Anthony, now eighteen years old, took part, following in his father's footsteps as one of the most talented jousters of his day. But Loveday was a hollow victory for Henry VI, for soon the lords began expressing their dissatisfaction with his rule all over again.

NOTES

[1] CPR 1446-1452, p. 205.
[2] TNA, E 101/410/11: Account of Edward Ellesmere, treasurer of the chamber and keeper of the jewels of Queen Margaret.

3 Joseph Stevenson (ed.), *Letters and Papers Illustrative of the Wars of the English in France During the Reign of Henry the Sixth, King of England*, Volume 2, Issue 2, p. 640.

4 Edward Hall, *Chronicle*, p. 219.

5 Roger Virgoe, *The Death of William de la Pole, Duke of Suffolk*, p. 491 n. 3.

6 *Memoirs of Sir Thomas More*, p. 218.

7 Philippa Gregory, David Baldwin, Michael Jones, *The Women of the Cousins' War: The Duchess, the Queen, and the King's Mother*, p. 155.

8 David Baldwin, *Elizabeth Woodville: Mother of the Princes in the Tower*, p. 157.

9 Ibid., p. 156.

10 Ibid., p. 155, 157.

11 Bertram Wolffe, *Henry VI*, p. 17.

12 Helen Maurer, *Delegitimizing Lancaster*, p. 173.

13 John Blacman, *Henry the Sixth: a Reprint of John Blacman's Memoir with Translation and Notes*, p. 29.

14 Amy Licence, *Cecily Neville: Mother of Kings*, p. 103.

15 John Blacman, *Henry the Sixth: a Reprint of John Blacman's Memoir with Translation and Notes*, p. 26.

16 A. R. Myers, (ed.), *English Historical Documents 1327-1485*, p. 259.

17 Bertram Wolffe, *Henry VI*, p. 18.

18 Basil Fulford Lowther Clarke, *Mental Disorder in Earlier Britain: Exploratory Studies*, p. 188.

19 Jean Froissart, *The Ancient Chronicles of Sir John Froissart, of England, France and Spain*, Volume 2, p. 201.

20 *Wethamsted's Register*, as cited in K. Dockray (ed.), *A Source Book*, p. 6.

21 *Collection of Ordinances*, p. 78.

22 *Three Catalogues Describing the Contents of the Red Book of the Exchequer*, p. 278.

23 Keith Dockray, *Sourcebook*, p. 145.

24 Diana Webb, *Pilgrims and Pilgrimage in the Medieval West* , p. 210.

25 *Calendar of State Papers and Manuscripts in the Archives and Collections of Milan 1385-1618*, n. 23.

26 *Paston Letters*, Volume 2, p. 534.

27 Kristen Geaman, A Bastard and a Changeling? *England's Edward of Westminster and Delayed Childbirth* in Valerie Schutte (ed.), *Unexpected Heirs in Early Modern Europe: Potential Kings and Queens*, p. 16.

28 Ibid., p. 17.

---

[29] *Coventry Leet Book*, p. 292.
[30] *The Paston Letters*, Volume 3, p. 75.
[31] *Coventry Leet Book*, p. 299.

CHAPTER 6:
WOMEN AT WAR

In 1459, the forces of Richard, Duke of York, Richard, Earl of Salisbury, and Richard, Earl of Warwick, met up at the Duke of York's stronghold, Ludlow Castle. They were actively preparing to take up arms against their King, Henry VI. Cecily Neville, who used to serve as Queen Margaret's lady-in-waiting, followed the unfolding events with bated breath, accompanied by her youngest children Margaret, George and Richard. The stakes were high, for if her husband won the battle, she would become Queen and her children heirs to the throne. But that evening the Earl of Warwick's senior commander, Sir Anthony Trollop, betrayed his trust and, under cover of darkness, journeyed to the King's camp and informed him of the plans. Fearing for his life, the Duke of York abandoned his military plans and escaped to Ireland, burning bridges as he went.

The Duchess of York and her children were abandoned at Ludlow, hoping that, according to the fifteenth century's chivalric code, the King would not hurt them. On 13 October 1459, Cecily awoke to the noise of hoofbeats. One chronicler reported that "King Harry rode into Ludlow, and spoiled the town and castle, whereat he found the Duchess of York with her two young sons".[1] Although the King was notoriously averse to war, his men looted the town and "defoulyd many women". Ludlow, Cecily's home, was "robbed to the bare walls", and the duchess herself was "unmanly and cruelly entreated and spoiled".[2] Some historians suggested that she was raped by Henry VI's men, but this, as pointed out by Cecily's recent biographer, seems unlikely.

Still, as the wife of a traitor, Cecily was treated harshly by the King's representatives. Henry VI decided to send her to the honourable custody of her sister Anne Stafford, Duchess of Buckingham, but Cecily could not hope for a favourable treatment there. She was "kept fully straight" and dealt "many a great rebuke" by the Duke of Buckingham, who was a loyal Lancastrian.[3]

On 20 November 1459, the "Parliament of Devils" convened at Coventry. Its chief aim was taking action against York, Salisbury and Warwick, who were branded as traitors to the crown. Although it was highly unusual to single women out, Cecily's sister-in-law Alice, Countess of Salisbury, was attainted for treason on the grounds that she had "imagined and compassed the King's death" and had "given advice and encouragement" to the Yorkist leaders.[4] Cecily may have feared similar treatment and decided to plead her case with the King.

In early December, Cecily was allowed to leave her house arrest and head towards Coventry to appeal directly to Henry VI, throwing herself and her children on his mercy. A contemporary account recorded Cecily's meeting with the King:

"The Duchess of York came unto King Harry and submitted her unto his grace, and she prayed for her husband that he might come to his answer and to be received unto his grace; and the King fully humbly granted her grace, and to all hers that would come with her, and to all other that would come in within eight days."[5]

Henry VI was not vindictive and granted Cecily and her children one thousand marks of annual income, as he perceived them as innocents who didn't offend him. Having settled Cecily's case, the King now turned to pursuing other traitors. Jacquetta Woodville's husband and eldest son, Anthony, were stationed at Sandwich when the King ordered them to aid Henry Beaufort, Duke of Somerset, (whose father had been executed at St Albans in 1455) against Richard Neville, Earl of Warwick, who occupied Calais.

On 19 January 1460, the royal fleet was unexpectedly attacked by Sir John Dynham, and the Woodville men were surprised in their beds. Jacquetta was with her husband when the surprise attack occurred, but she was spared the humiliation that Warwick had prepared for her husband and son at Calais.[6] One of the Paston correspondents wrote in January 1460 that "my lady Duchess is still again received in Kent", which means that Jacquetta's gender protected her from being humiliated by Warwick.[7]

Richard Woodville represented the King and called the Earls of Warwick and Salisbury traitors. This so enraged Salisbury that he berated Richard, calling him a "knave's son, that he should be so rude to call him and these other lords traitors, for they shall be found the King's true liege men". If anyone was a traitor, Salisbury ranted, it was Richard himself. Warwick joined in and told Richard that "his father was but a squire, and brought up with King Henry V, and he himself was made by marriage, and also made Lord, and that it was not his part to have such language of lords, being of the King's blood".[8] The Duke of

York's son, Edward, Earl of March, was also present and "rated him in likewise". Anthony, Jacquetta's son, was similarly abused. Salisbury and Warwick were highly sensitive about their status as great lords and loathed Richard Woodville because they believed the King favoured him because of his marriage to Jacquetta. Their comments highlight the fact that Jacquetta was perceived as influential enough for her husband to be berated as "made by marriage" to her.

On 10 July 1460, Richard, Earl of Warwick, scored a victory against Henry VI's army during the Battle of Northampton and took possession of the King's person. Many of the King's loyal supporters died that day, including Humphrey Stafford, Duke of Buckingham, in whose household Cecily, Duchess of York, was kept under house arrest. The King was solemnly escorted to London, with Warwick carrying a sword in front of him as a sign of reverence and kingly honour. Rumours abounded. The Milanese ambassador reported that the coalition of York, Salisbury and Warwick planned the change of regime; "they will make a son of the Duke of York king, and they will pass over the King's son, as they are beginning already to say that he is not the King's son".[9] These developments frightened Queen Margaret, who escaped with her son to Wales.

In September 1460, Richard, Duke of York, returned from Ireland and made his own bid for the throne. He was no longer interested in reforming the existing government: his main goal was to become King himself. During York's procession towards Westminster, he adopted the trappings of royalty, having a royal coat of arms and naked sword carried in front of him. He also summoned his wife, Cecily, who was released from house arrest shortly after the victory at Northampton. She joined him and travelled in great pomp in a chariot covered with blue velvet drawn by eight coursers.

Once York reached Westminster, he went to the Presence Chamber of the palace, where the King's throne stood under the canopy of estate. York approached it and "claimed the sole right of sitting upon it" and produced a genealogy tracing his lineage to Lionel, Duke of Clarence, "to whose successors, he asserted, the kingdom of England rightly belonged, since he was the elder [son of Edward III], rather than to the descendants of John Duke of Lancaster, the younger [brother of Lionel] from whom King Henry was descended. York also protested that "he would no longer endure the injustices which the three Henrys, who were usurpers, had for so long inflicted upon his line".[10] He then "entered the inner rooms of the palace" and gave orders to remove Henry VI from his apartments.

The King was sent to the Queen's side of the palace while York claimed the King's rooms. When asked if he wished to see the King, York said: "I do not recall that I know anyone in the kingdom whom it would not benefit to come to me and see my person, rather than I should and visit him." It was all clear: York had usurped the King's place.

But the lords hesitated. It was one thing to reform the kingdom and quite another to claim the throne for himself. They baulked at the idea of York becoming King and decided to resolve the matter differently. On 24 October 1460, the Act of Accord passed in Parliament proclaiming York as Henry VI's rightful heir. Henry, it was stipulated, would remain King for the rest of his life, and York and his heirs would succeed him after his death. The King's son, Prince Edward, was bypassed since York had spread rumours that he was not Henry's son, but Margaret's bastard. It was not quite what York was hoping to achieve, but it was better than nothing.

On the night of 31 October 1460, the King was removed "against his own will" from Westminster to the Bishop of London's palace, where York came to him by torchlight, "behaving as if he were king, and said in many places that 'this is ours by very right'".[11] Margaret of Anjou was in Wales at the time, where she had escaped with her son and a small retinue. One of her servants "plundered and robbed her, and put her in doubt of her life and her son's life also".[12] Evading Yorkist scouts, the Queen made an arduous journey to Harlech Castle, the seat of Henry VI's half brother Jasper Tudor.

The King loved his two half brothers, took care of their education and had them ennobled in 1452. They were the sons of Catherine of Valois and her secretly wedded husband, Owen Tudor. Edmund, the older Tudor, received the earldom of Richmond while Jasper, the younger, became the Earl of Pembroke. In 1455, Edmund married twelve-year-old Margaret Beaufort, the sole heiress of John Beaufort, first Duke of Somerset. Edmund died in November 1456; his young wife gave birth to his son, Henry, on 28 January 1457. This little boy would one day inherit England's crown as Henry VII.

Jasper was fiercely loyal to Henry VI and sheltered the Queen and Prince Edward, offering them succour and military assistance. The Queen sent for her royal supporters, including the Duke of Somerset and the Earl of Devon, and amassed an army of fifteen thousand men. The Queen also sought foreign assistance. She spent the Christmas festivities of 1460 in Scotland as a guest of Queen Mary of Guelders, who served as regent for her eight-year-old son James III.

Margaret was still in Scotland when her army, led by Henry Beaufort, Duke of Somerset, met with the Duke of York's army at Wakefield. York and his son Edmund, Earl of Rutland, were slain on the battlefield on 30 December 1460. York's sidekick, the Earl of Salisbury, was executed at Pontefract, where York's body was posthumously decapitated. His head, adorned with a paper crown in derision of his royal aspirations, was placed over Micklegate Bar at York.

As soon as she learned of York's death, Margaret of Anjou left Scotland and headed to York, "where, by the counsel of the lords, it was decided to march with all possible strength to London and rescue King Henry from the hands of his enemies".[13] Her army included "Frenchmen and Bretons, and Irish men". In later years, according to

Pope Pius II, Margaret took up the role of a military leader and spoke in front of her armies, saying: "I have often broken their [the English] battle line. I have mowed down ranks far more stubborn than theirs are now. You who once followed a peasant girl [Joan of Arc], follow now a queen." If the battle went against them, she said: "I will either conquer or be conquered with you." The men "marvelled at such boldness in a woman, at a man's courage in a woman's breast, and at her reasonable arguments".[14]

But if Margaret thought York's death would put an end to her troubles, she was mistaken. York's cause was taken up by his eldest son, Edward, Earl of March, who now styled himself Duke of York. On 2 February 1461, he met Margaret's army, led by Jasper Tudor and his father, Owen, at Mortimer's Cross, where he scored victory. In an act of retribution for his father's death, Edward executed the King's stepfather, Owen Tudor.

It was at Mortimer's Cross that "three suns shining" appeared in the sky. It was taken as a sign that God favoured the Yorkist cause, and Edward himself thought so, kneeling down and praying fervently. In reality, the three suns that he saw was an atmospheric optical phenomenon that consists of a bright spot to one or both sides of the sun.

In London, Cecily, Duchess of York, was frightened when she learned that Margaret of Anjou's army was coming. A battle was inevitable as Richard, Earl of Warwick, headed towards the town of St Albans, and any outcome was possible. Among the casualties of the recent wars were Cecily's husband, son and brother, and she was naturally afraid that violence would erupt once the Queen's army reached London. Apart from Edward, Cecily had two more sons, George and Richard, whom she sent to Burgundy, accompanied by a female servant, Alice Martyn.

Taking the King with him, Warwick reached St Albans where, on 17 February 1461, the Queen's army scored victory. Warwick fled from the battlefield and left the King with a small company behind, losing his precious royal hostage. Prospero di Camulio, Milanese ambassador at the French court, reported that "the King was placed under a tree a mile away, where he laughed and sang".[15] Jehan de Waurin reported something similar, writing that "the King was taken under a great oak, where he was laughing greatly at what had occurred".[16] This has often been interpreted by historians as Henry's madness manifesting itself once again, but his recent biographer suggested that these two reports referred to the King chanting prayers for the safe deliverance of his wife and son.[17]

One contemporary chronicler reported that Henry VI "took his field beside a little town called Sandridge, not far from St Albans, in a place called 'No-man's-land', and there he stood and saw his people slain on both sides".[18] Contemporary sources relating the battle make it clear that although Henry was present near the battlefield, he didn't take a direct part in the fighting. Usually, kings had armed bodyguards and standard bearers guarding them during battles, but Henry had only two guardians, Lords Bonville and Kyriell, who were executed afterwards. With a whiff of contempt, the author of *Gregory's Chronicle* stated that "in the middle of the battle King Harry went unto his Queen and forsook all his lords, and trusted better to her party than unto his own lords".[19] The Lancastrian royal family was reunited, and in the evening the King knighted his son.

The Lancastrian army now intended to march on London. News had already spread that the Queen's army was looting, pillaging and raping on its way to the capital. Richard Lee, Lord Mayor of London, and the Common Council turned to women to help protect the city. Exploiting the long-term friendship between Jacquetta Woodville and

Margaret of Anjou, the Lord Mayor sent the Duchess of Bedford to intervene on the city's behalf: "The Duchess of Bedford and the Lady Scales, with divers clerks and curates of the City, went to St Albans to the King, Queen, and the Prince, for to entreat for grace for the City."[20] The Milanese ambassador reported that Jacquetta, whom he referred to as "my Lady the Regent", identifying her still as the Duke of Bedford's widow, was accompanied by Anne Stafford, Duchess of Buckingham. The women returned to London on 20 February, reporting that "the King and Queen had no mind to pillage the chief city and chamber of their realm, and so they promised; but at the same time they did not mean that they would not punish the evildoers."[21]

In retrospect, Margaret of Anjou's decision not to enter London was her biggest mistake, for on 4 March 1461 Edward, Earl of March, entered the city and proclaimed himself Edward IV, King of England. Edward set up his temporary court at Baynards Castle, his mother's London residence. Before he left the city, he gathered "all the notables of London" and "recommended them to the duchess his mother".[22] Cecily's house now became the centre of power and source of information about Edward's whereabouts.

On 29 March 1461, Edward scored a victory against Henry VI and Margaret of Anjou's army at Towton. It was one of the bloodiest, most vicious battles fought on English soil, with an estimated fifty thousand soldiers fighting for hours amidst a snowstorm on that day. Cecily, Duchess of York, received news of her son's victory at 11:00 a.m. on Easter Eve, 4 April 1461. The letter bore Edward IV's sign-manual. One of the letters in the Paston correspondence, written by William to his brother John, summarized its contents, writing: "First, our sovereign lord hath won the field, and upon the Monday next after Palm Sunday he was received into York with great solemnity and processions."[23]

Jacquetta Woodville's husband headed a force of some seven thousand Welshmen against Edward and was captured, along with his eldest son, Anthony, and promptly sent to the Tower of London. William Paston wrote incorrectly that Anthony was killed at Towton. He described him as "Lord Scales", which attests that by the time the letter was written on 4 April 1461, Anthony was already a married man.[24] His wife was Elizabeth, the daughter and sole heiress of Thomas Scales, Baron Scales.

Cecily, as mother of the new King, was now the most powerful woman in the kingdom. From the letter of her son,

Cecily learned that Henry VI, Margaret of Anjou and their son, Prince Edward, fled to Scotland, accompanied by the Duke of Somerset, the Duke of Exeter and Lord Roos, but were "chased and followed" by Edward IV.[25] On Easter Monday, Nicholas O'Flanagan, Bishop of Elphin, visited Baynards Castle and wrote a letter to papal nuncio Francesco Coppini:

"Moreover at the hour of vespers, on the second feast of Easter week, I was present in the house of the Duchess of York. Immediately after vespers the Lord Treasurer came to her with an authentic letter stating that the late King with his kindred and those mentioned above, had all been taken and brought to King Edward. Because of this news the duchess returned again to the chapel with two chaplains and myself, and there we said *Te Deum*; after which I told her that the time had come for writing to your lordship, of which she approved."[26]

Cecily emerged as the power behind the throne, as is evident from the bishop's advice to Coppini: "As soon as you can, send letters to the King, the Chancellor and other lords, because I see that it would please them, write also to the duchess, who has a great regard for you, and can rule the king as she pleases".[27] Two weeks later Coppini's physician gave the nuncio a similar piece of advice, writing:

"Your lordship must decide whether you will change your mind about writing, or if you wish me to go to England with the information and letters which you delivered to me, although, in my opinion, your lordship should write to those whom you think best to offer congratulations on the victory, advising me of what you wish me to do in general and in special with the King, and in congratulating the lords, your friends, and well-wishers, not forgetting, on any account, to write to the Duchess of York or to Nettunen, because he is good."[28]

At the height of her power, Cecily could now send for her two younger sons, George and Richard, who were feted by Philip the Good, Duke of Burgundy, in Bruges. Talk was already underway about a possible Anglo-Burgundian marriage alliance between either George or Richard and the duke's four-year-old granddaughter Mary:

"It is reported among the English lords that the Duke of Burgundy is treating the brothers of the King with respect. This pleases them wonderfully, and they believe that there will be great friendship between the duke and the English by an indissoluble treaty, and that one of these brothers will marry the daughter of Charles. I gather from what the Bishop of Salisbury says that he would like the duke and his council to write to him specially, as the King's privy councillor, for what is to be done between them, and by their diligence he intends to labour with effect."[29]

But before he could turn his attention to planning marriages for himself and his brothers, Edward IV had to deal with Henry VI and Margaret of Anjou, who were sheltering in Scotland. Writing to James III soon after their escape, Edward requested the extradition of Henry, Margaret and their son:

"Whereas you took and received unto your land our traitors and rebels, Harry, late usurpant king of our said realm, Margaret his wife, and her son, and other our traitors and rebels, not being your liegemen; omitting thereby the duty of the state and the worship that ye should bear to the noble princehood. We exhort and require you, in God's behalf, to deliver unto us without delay our said traitor and rebels, if they become not your lieges and subjects; and if it so be, to certify us the same under seal; showing yourself unto us in these, as in like case ye would we or any other prince should show them to you."[30]

In the aftermath of Henry VI's defeat, various rumours started circulating in England and abroad. The Milanese ambassador Prospero di Camulio reported in

March 1461 that rumours of abdication were repeated at court:

"They say here that the Queen of England, after the King had abdicated in favour of his son, gave the King poison. At least he has known how to die, if he did not know what to do else. It is said that the Queen will unite with the Duke of Somerset. However these are rumours in which I do not repose much confidence."[31]

Camulio was right to be sceptical about these reports. In his next dispatch, the ambassador repeated that it was said in England that Henry VI "had resigned his crown in favour of his son, although they say his Majesty remarked at another time, that he must be the son of the Holy Spirit". Camulio's remark is often quoted by historians as evidence that Henry believed Prince Edward was not his son, but it's a mistake to believe he ever said any such thing. Camulio dismissed the rumour, writing that "these may only be the words of common fanatics, such as they have at present in that island".[32] Indeed, Henry always believed Edward of Westminster to be his son and clearly had affection for both his wife and their only child. The illegitimacy rumour, started by the Yorkists in the 1450s, was used to smear Margaret of Anjou's name. Edward IV continued the Yorkist campaign of impugning Margaret's virtue and referred to Prince Edward of Westminster as "her son" rather than the King's.[33]

With the Lancastrian royal family gone, Jacquetta Woodville and her family had to make an important decision: Should they still support the Lancastrian cause or turn to the victorious King Edward? The Milanese ambassador at the English court, Count Dallugo, wrote that the Woodvilles offered their allegiance to Edward IV: "The lords adherent to King Henry are all quitting him, and come to tender obedience to this king, and at this present one of the chief of them has come, by name Lord de Rivers, with one of his sons, men of very great valor".[34] "I held several conversations with this Lord de Rivers about King Henry's cause, and what he thought of it", Dallugo wrote to Francesco Sforza, Duke of Milan. Richard was blunt with the ambassador and replied that the Lancastrian cause "was lost irretrievably". What Jacquetta thought of it remains unknown, but she certainly shared her husband's opinion.

The Woodvilles' change of allegiance paid off; writing from Stony Stratford in the spring of 1461, Edward IV informed his cousin Bishop George Neville that "he had decided to pardon, remit and forgive Lord Rivers, of all manner of offences and trespasses of him done against us".[35] Jacquetta's husband received his pardon on 12 July 1461, and their eldest son, Anthony, was pardoned on 23 July. Another Woodville son, Richard, was pardoned on 8 February 1462. What role Jacquetta played in these pardons remains obscure, but the Burgundian chronicler Jehan de Waurin suggested that Edward IV pardoned the Woodvilles when he met Jacquetta's eldest daughter, Elizabeth, and fell in love with her.[36]

Elizabeth Grey was among many young women whose lives were affected by the wars. On 17 February 1461, she lost her husband, who was killed at St Albans. They had two small sons, Thomas and Richard. It's possible that Elizabeth took up residence with her mother following her husband's death. As would soon become apparent, Edward IV wanted to make Elizabeth his mistress. Elizabeth, however, was as virtuous as she was beautiful and refused to become the King's paramour. The consequences of her refusal would change her family's future and alter the course of history.

NOTES

1 John Allen Giles, *The Chronicles of the White Rose of York: A Series of Historical Fragments*, p. 5.
2 J. L. Laynesmith, *Cecily Duchess of York*, p. 70.
3 Ibid., p. 71.

4 Gwen Seabourne, *Imprisoning Medieval Women*, p. 31.

5 Ibid., p. 72.

6 Her presence is mentioned in *Gregory's Chronicle*, p. 206.

7 James Gairdner (ed.), *The Paston Letters A.D. 1422-1509*, p. 203. Editor of the Paston letters identified the "lady duchess" as Cecily, Duchess of York, but the context makes it clear that it was Jacquetta, not Cecily.

8 Ibid., p. 204.

9 *Calendar of State Papers , Milan, 1385-1618*, n. 38.

10 Keith Dockray, *Henry VI, Margaret of Anjou and the Wars of the Roses*, p. 165.

11 Ibid., p. 166.

12 Ibid.

13 Keith Dockray, p. 172.

14 Ibid., p. 77.

15 *Calendar of State Papers and Manuscripts in the Archives and Collections of Milan 1385-1618*, n. 71.

16 F. H. Durham, *English History Illustrated from Original Sources*, p. 42.

17 Lauren Johnson, *Shadow King: The Life and Death of Henry VI* p. 436.

18 John Silvester Davies (ed.), *An English Chronicle*, p. 107.

19 James Gairdner (ed.), *The Historical Collections of a Citizen of London in the Fifteenth Century*, Volume 17, p. 212.

20 Arlene Okerlund, *Elizabeth Woodville*, p. 55.

21 *Calendar of State Papers, Milan 1385-1618*, n. 65.

22 Norman Davies, *Paston Letters and Papers of the Fifteenth Century*, Part 1, p. 165.

23 Ibid.

24 Ibid.

25 Ibid.

26 *Calendar of State Papers and Manuscripts in the Archives and Collections of Milan 1385-1618*, n. 81.

27 Ibid.

28 Ibid., n. 88.

29 Ibid., n. 82.

30 James Orchard Halliwell, *Letters of the Kings of England*, pp. 125-126.

31 *Calendar of State Papers and Manuscripts in the Archives and Collections of Milan 1385-1618*, n. 75.

32 Ibid., n. 76.

33 James Orchard Halliwell, *Letters of the Kings of England*, pp. 125-126.

34 *Calendar of State Papers, Milan 1385-1618*, n. 120.

35 Cora Scofield, *Edward the Fourth*, Volume 1, p. 178.

---

[36] *Recueil des croniques et anchiennes istories de la Grant Bretaigne*, p. 352.

CHAPTER 7:
THE NEW ROYAL FAMILY

Edward IV was ardent in his pursuit of Jacquetta's daughter, but Elizabeth would not agree to be a royal mistress since she had heard about his reputation as a womaniser and sought to disassociate herself from wanton behaviour. Edward was a "lusty prince" who "had attempted the stability and constant modesty of diverse ladies and gentlewomen". Taking advantage of his good looks, charisma and the royal aura that surrounded him, Edward "pursued with no discrimination the married and unmarried, the noble and the lowly . . . he overcame all by money and promises, and having conquered them, he dismissed them".[1] Elizabeth had no intention of being dismissed in disgrace and was wary of Edward's attentions. But Edward would not take no for an answer and decided to overcome Elizabeth's reluctance by force, or so it was reported some twenty years later by an Italian visitor to England, Dominic Mancini:

"The story runs that when Edward placed a dagger at her throat, to make her submit to his passion, she remained unperturbed and determined to die rather than live unchastely with the king. Whereupon Edward coveted her much the more, and he judged the lady worthy to be a royal spouse who could not be overcome in her constancy even by an infatuated king."[2]

The contemporary Italian poet Antonio Cornazzano suggested that it was Elizabeth who held the knife to her throat and said she would rather kill herself than "live in eternal filth and squalor" as a discarded royal mistress.[3] It is possible that Elizabeth refused Edward because she was offended that he had berated her father and brother for their lowly origin in 1460; she defiantly informed the King that "though too humble to be his wife, she was too high to become his concubine".[4] But instead of discouraging him, Elizabeth's refusal triggered Edward's ardour, and he fell madly in love with her. The young King finally realised that he "could not corrupt her virtue by gifts or menaces" and decided to marry her instead.[5]

Romantic legend surrounds the courtship of Edward IV and Elizabeth Woodville. The Victorian historian Agnes Strickland placed their very first meeting under an oak tree, where Elizabeth "addressed the young monarch, holding her fatherless boys by the hands, and when Edward paused to listen to her, she threw herself at his feet and pleaded earnestly for the restoration of Bradgate, the inheritance of her children". Strickland adds that the tree, known as "the Queen's Oak", "was the scene of more than one interview between the beautiful Elizabeth and the enamoured Edward" and gave the direct location: "between Grafton and the Whittlebury Forest".[6] Today, the legend still lives on and "the Queen's Oak", although it is probably not the same tree that stood tall in the 1460s, is found between Potterspury and Grafton Regis.

The oak tree story seems like a romantic fabrication. The couple likely met for the first time in the early 1460s, when Elizabeth's father and brothers were pardoned for their Lancastrian sympathies. There might be some truth in Thomas More's story that Elizabeth "made a humble suit unto the King that she might be restored unto such small lands as her late husband had given her in jointure".[7] In 1463, Elizabeth's father became Edward's councillor, so she would have had plenty of opportunities to visit court and plead her case with the King, although it's also likely that she didn't approach Edward IV directly.

A document signed on 13 April 1464 sheds more light on whom Elizabeth approached. She chose William, Lord Hastings, the King's loyal long-term friend and companion. In their mutually signed contract, they agreed that Elizabeth's elder son, or his younger brother, Richard, in the event of Thomas Grey's death, would marry one of Hastings's daughters or nieces. If Thomas or Richard Grey were ever able to recover some of their father's ancestral lands, or any of the inheritance of their grandmother Lady Ferrers of Groby, the contract obliged them to divide profits between themselves, Lord Hastings and Elizabeth. The contract never came to fruition, however, as Elizabeth soon found a husband who was able to take care of her financially.[8]

It is traditionally believed that Edward IV married Elizabeth Woodville on 1 May 1464. The date had long been associated with love, possibly originating from pre-Christian traditional celebrations of fertility.[9] It's likely, however, that the date is symbolic and was put forward to associate Edward IV's marriage with pagan practises and thus diminish its importance or question its validity. It seems unlikely that Elizabeth would have entered into a bargain with Lord Hastings in April 1464 had she known that the King of England wanted to marry her. Also, in August 1464 William Hastings was granted wardship of Elizabeth's older son Thomas, and it's unlikely that Hastings would have received such a grant if Elizabeth was already married to the King. It is more likely that Edward married

Elizabeth shortly before he announced their match in Reading in September 1464.

Just how the match came about seems unclear. Chronicler Edward Hall recounted how the King was hunting in the forest near Stony Stratford in the spring of 1464. Tiring his horses, he "came for his recreation to the manor of Grafton, where the Duchess of Bedford sojourned, then wife to Sir Richard Woodville, lord Rivers, on whom then was attending a daughter of hers, called Elizabeth Grey".[10] There, he fell in love with Elizabeth and married her.

Chroniclers often ascribe Edward's decision to marry Elizabeth to the spur of the moment, but other, better-informed sources claimed that it took some time for Edward to win Elizabeth over. A letter from October 1464 suggests that Edward IV "has determined to take [as a wife] the daughter of my Lord de Rivers, a widow with two children, having long loved her, it appears".[11] The contemporary chronicle stated that the King fell in love with Elizabeth when he "dined with her frequently", and Thomas More, although born in 1478 and not a contemporary to these events, confirmed this when he wrote that "many a meeting, much wooing, and many great promises" were involved in the courtship.[12]

The clandestine nature of Edward IV's marriage led Richard III's Parliament to claim in 1483 that the wedding was procured "by sorcery and witchcraft, committed by the said Elizabeth and her mother, Jacquetta, Duchess of Bedford".[13] According to the act, witchcraft committed by Elizabeth and Jacquetta was "the common opinion of the people and the public voice, and the fame is through all this land".[14] Witchcraft was often used as a means of slandering powerful women, and this was also the case with Jacquetta and her daughter. But the fact that Jacquetta played a pivotal role in Elizabeth's clandestine marriage was stressed by contemporary chronicler Fabyan, who wrote that:

"In most secret manner, upon the first day of May, King Edward espoused Elizabeth, late wife of Sir John Grey, knight, which before time was slain at Towton of York field, which espousals were solemnised early in the morning at a town named Grafton, near Stony Stratford; at which marriage was no persons present but the spouse, the spousess, the duchess of Bedford her mother, the priest, two gentlewomen and a young man to help the priest sing."[15]

Jacquetta further ensured that the marriage was consummated so that it could not be annulled. After the ceremony, Elizabeth "nightly to his [Edward's] bed was brought, in so secret manner that almost none but her mother was of counsel".[16] The chronicler's words suggest that the King may have spent some time at Elizabeth's residence, and since she was said to have resided with her mother, this residence was the Woodvilles' ancestral seat at Grafton. It's possible that the marriage took place in the Hermitage Chapel on Woodville land rather than in the Church of St Mary the Virgin in the village of Grafton Regis, hence later accusations that the wedding was secretive. The site of the hermitage was excavated in 1965, and a number of fifteenth-century floor tiles decorated with the white roses of York and Woodville coat of arms was unearthed, "indicating that the building was significant for both families".[17]

It appears that Jacquetta did all that was in her power to ensure that her daughter would not be dishonoured and later discarded; although the marriage was conducted in great secrecy, there were five witnesses, including Jacquetta herself, so Edward could not have denied it. But if Jacquetta thought her illustrious royal lineage would bolster her daughter's eligibility as Edward's bride, she was very much mistaken, for when the news of the marriage leaked, a great scandal erupted.

"The greater part of the lords and the people in general seem very much dissatisfied at this" and tried to find "means to annul it", wrote the Milanese ambassador in October 1464.[18] The Burgundian chronicler Jehan de Waurin reported that when Edward finally admitted to having married Elizabeth in September 1464 at Reading Abbey, his nobles informed him that "she was not his match, that however good and fair she might be, she was not a wife for so high a prince as he; and he knew this well, for she was not the daughter of a duke or earl, but her mother had married a simple knight, so that though she was the daughter of the Duchess of Bedford and the niece of the Count of Saint-Pol, she was no wife for him".[19]

Edward IV's announcement of his marriage sent shockwaves across England, but most stunned of all was his mother, Cecily Neville. Had her husband survived, she would have been Queen of England and she hoped that she would at least exert a role similar to a Queen mother. When she learned that Edward had married Elizabeth Woodville, she was horrified. There are two sources describing Cecily's reaction. First was written almost twenty years after the

King's marriage by Dominic Mancini, who asserted that Cecily "fell into such a frenzy, that she offered to submit to a public inquiry and asserted that Edward was not the offspring of her husband the Duke of York, but was conceived in adultery, and therefore in no wise worthy of the honour of kingship".[20] If Cecily ever said such a thing, casting a shadow of doubt on her own reputation, this would come back to haunt her in the years to come. Another account, by Sir Thomas More writing in the sixteenth century, minutely describes Cecily's conversation with Edward and the arguments she used to convey her displeasure. She was "so sore moved therewith that she argued against the marriage as much as she possibly might, alleging that it was in his honour, profit, and surety also, to marry in a noble progeny out of his realm".

Cecily raised an important issue, pointing out that by marrying his subject Edward had effectively robbed England of concluding a prestigious marriage alliance. Cecily said that "it was not princely to marry his own subject, no great occasion leading thereunto, no possessions, or other commodities depending thereupon". Foreign princesses came with large dowries and the promise of matrimonial alliances. There was also another issue: Edward, a young and inexperienced king, ascended to the throne by sheer accident; had his father survived Wakefield, he would most likely be the king. Cecily always described herself as "queen by right", emphasising that she came very close to becoming Queen consort, but now her son had taken a mere commoner as his wife. She also pointed out that the Earl of Warwick, who had played a pivotal role in setting the crown on Edward's head, was busy negotiating a marriage alliance with Bona of Savoy. Warwick "had so far moved already", Cecily argued, and was "not likely to take it well, if all his voyage were in such ways frustrated and his agreements dashed".

Cecily said that "there was nothing to be disliked" about Elizabeth Woodville, but there was also "nothing so excellent, but it might be found in diverse others that were more suitable". Elizabeth, Cecily argued, was a widow and not a virgin, and by marrying a woman who had already given her maidenhead to someone else, Edward put "a very blemish and high disparagement to the sacred majesty of a prince". Yet Edward was not to be crossed and informed his mother—"part in earnest, part in play merrily"—that he was "out of her rule". True, he would have been "glad if she should take it well", yet "to him it seemed that this marriage, even worldly considered, was not unprofitable". Alliances could be brokered at any time, and he would "find the means to enter thereinto". Edward didn't doubt that there were other women comparable with Elizabeth, but he wanted none of them. As to his cousin, the Earl of Warwick, he believed that Warwick would be happy for him, but he would not be "ruled by his eye than by mine own, as though I were a child that were bound to marry by the appointment of a guardian". Edward knew that Warwick had played a pivotal role in his accession, but he emphasised that "I would not be a king with that condition—to give up mine own liberty in the choice of my own marriage".

As to Elizabeth being a widow with two small sons, Edward said that this was an advantage rather than an obstacle. Since he was a bachelor who had already sired illegitimate children, "each of us has a proof that neither of us is like to be barren". "And therefore, Madam, I pray you be content", Edward urged his mother. Trying to sweeten the pill, Edward also said: "I trust in God she shall bring forth a young prince that shall please you."[21]

Yet Cecily was still not appeased and pointed out that Edward should rather marry "one Dame Elizabeth Lucy, whom the King had also not long before gotten with child". Cecily then "objected openly against his marriage, as it were in discharge of her conscience" because she believed "that the King was betrothed to Dame Elizabeth Lucy, and (was) her husband before God". The lady in question was sent for and examined, and swore that she and the King "were never betrothed". Elizabeth Lucy was the daughter of Thomas Wayte from Hampshire, who married into the Lucy family.[22] She was the mother of Edward IV's illegitimate son Arthur Plantagenet (later known as Viscount Lisle), who came into prominence during the reign of Henry VIII.

A story about Edward IV's amorous pursuits may have been circulating at the time, and it's likely that Elizabeth Woodville refused to become a royal mistress precisely because she didn't want to join the ranks of women seduced by Edward IV. In 1483, another woman's name would be linked to Edward IV and the story of pre-contract; he was said to have married Eleanor Butler before pursuing Elizabeth. How much Elizabeth knew about Edward's pre-contract, if it ever existed, remains unknown, but the issue would eventually come back to haunt her after Edward's death.[23]

Although Elizabeth Woodville was the daughter of a mere knight, she adopted a coat of arms prominently incorporating her mother's Saint-Pol connections and emphasising their Continental ancestry. If her lineage was not enough to render her suitable as Edward IV's consort, Elizabeth Woodville at least had the good looks to recommend her. Her portrait is now located in the Queens' College, Cambridge, and it is believed to have been derived in the sixteenth century from a lost original. The original portrait of Elizabeth, likely derived from a live sitting, was listed in the Royal Collection in 1542 and 1547—Henry VIII and Edward VI owned a portrait of Elizabeth, and it is highly likely that it was the original painting.[24] In the portrait, Elizabeth wears a black gown with patterned collar and cuffs, a truncated hennin and a matching necklace. Medieval fashion favoured displaying a high forehead, and many women plucked their eyebrows and the hair on their foreheads and temples to make their faces appear longer; Elizabeth clearly followed this fashion.

Apart from the portrait, of which many copies exist, there are also three contemporary miniatures depicting Elizabeth Woodville, albeit her face appears generic in each of them. A coronation portrait of Elizabeth in the *Illuminated Books of the Fraternity of Our Lady's Assumption of the Skinners' Company* depicts her wearing a red coronation surcoat trimmed with ermine. Over her shoulders, she wears a long blue coronation gown clasped at the décolletage with two brooches in the shape of gillyflowers. She wears a crown, holds an orb and a sceptre and her long blond hair flows down her back. Another illustration of Elizabeth as Queen can be found in the *Luton Guild Book*, which depicts her among the founding members of the Fraternity of the Holy and Undivided Trinity and Blessed Virgin Mary. Elizabeth and Edward kneel on either side of Bishop Rotherham before the Trinity and wear matching purple cloaks trimmed with ermine. The colour scheme of their gowns is also similar and appears to be cloth of gold; Elizabeth wears a rich, close-fitting Burgundian-style dress with blue motifs embroidered on it. She is flanked by her mother-in-law, Cecily, Duchess of York, and five ladies-in-waiting, all piously clasping their hands in prayer. In Lambeth Palace's copy of *The Dictes and Sayings of the Philosophers*, there is another illustration of the royal family showing Elizabeth's brother Anthony kneeling as he presents the King and Queen with a copy of his translated work. Here again the Queen is depicted with her long blond hair loose, wearing a crown and blue cloak trimmed with ermine.

Apart from contemporary miniature illustrations and the portrait derived from a lost original, there are also representations of Elizabeth Woodville in stained glass. The eastern window in the Little Malvern Priory depicts the family of Edward IV, including Elizabeth and their children. The upper section of the Queen's figure, however, has been lost during the course of history. Stained glass in the Canterbury Cathedral depicts Elizabeth, Edward IV and their children again—this particular representation of the Queen has been dated to 1482 and has survived to our time.

Dominic Mancini, who visited England in the summer of 1483, mentioned Elizabeth's "beauty of person and charm of manner" without getting into the details of her personal appearance. Another contemporary chronicler commented upon Elizabeth's "constant womanhood, wisdom and beauty",[25] although he, too, offered no details. Thomas More, a Tudor scholar and humanist who was writing some twenty years after Elizabeth Woodville's death, stated that she was "both fair and of a good favour, moderate of stature, well made and very wise".[26] Edward Hall, who started writing his chronicle in 1535, broke the mould when he stated that Elizabeth "was a woman more of formal countenance, than of excellent beauty, but yet of such fresh beauty and favour, that with her sober demeanour, lovely looking, and feminine smiling (neither too wanton nor too humble)... she allured and made subject to her the heart of so great a King".[27]

The new royal couple must have appeared dazzling together, as Edward IV was handsome, "of imposing build, taller than others".[28] His skeleton, examined in 1789, confirms this since the King was found to have stood some six foot three and a half inches tall. In the miniatures wherein he is depicted with Elizabeth, he has black hair and a swarthy complexion. Almost since the beginning of his reign, Edward adorned himself with costly garments, emphasising his newly acquired royal title with materials and colours reserved for royalty. He made sure that his court was to be among the most splendid in the entire Christendom.

In May 1465, Edward arranged for Elizabeth's coronation. As the Queen's mother, Jacquetta was prominent during the ceremonies, following in her daughter's wake and holding the long train of her gown. She also invited her brother Jacques de Luxembourg, Count of Saint-Pol, who represented his overlord, the Duke of Burgundy, and demonstrated to the English people that the Woodville Queen had powerful international connections and was not as lowly born as some would believe. The Count of Saint-Pol's presence at his niece's coronation attests that any ill feelings at Jacquetta's remarriage were long gone and that the siblings were reconciled.

Conspicuously absent from the new Queen's coronation was Richard Neville, Earl of Warwick, who found it difficult to accept Elizabeth Woodville's social elevation. News of Warwick's distaste spread in France, where Margaret of Anjou resided:

"The Queen, wife of King Henry, has written to the king here that she is advised that King Edward and the Earl of Warwick have come to very great division and war together. She begs the king here to be pleased to give her help so that she may be able to recover her kingdom or at least allow her to receive assistance from the lords of this kingdom who are willing to afford this, and if he will not take any one of these courses, she writes that she will take the best course that she can."[29]

"Look how proudly she writes", Louis XII remarked to one of the Milanese ambassadors at his court.[30] Over the past years, Margaret had sought Louis's help and even promised to surrender Calais to him in exchange for his help, but Margaret's hopes of enlisting the aid of the French were dashed because Louis sought a settlement with the Dukes of Burgundy and Brittany. Edward IV agreed to a truce at Hesdin on 8 October 1463, by which Louis renounced all aid to Henry VI and Margaret of Anjou.

Shortly after Elizabeth's coronation, Henry VI was captured in Clitherwood, accompanied only by two chaplains and a young squire. He was brought to London on horseback on 24 June 1465, his feet tied to the stirrups. Edward IV promptly sent his rival to the Tower of London, wherein Henry VI would spend the next five years of his life. According to Henry's biographer and friend John Blacman, the King "patiently endured hunger, thirst, mockings, derisions, abuse, and many other hardships".[31] But Blacman's account was not factual history; he was pushing for Henry VI to be canonised as a saint and was writing a hagiography detailing how the King patiently endured mistreatment in imitation of Christ and how he experienced religious visions while in the Tower.

Edward IV's accounts show that Henry VI was treated well during his imprisonment. Edward employed five members of his own household to attend on "Henry of Windsor", as Henry VI was referred to in the rolls. There were as many as twenty-two servants attending Henry, and five marks were assigned for his weekly maintenance. He received wine from Edward IV's cellars and velvet from the royal wardrobe for his clothes.[32] Far from secluded in a dungeon, Henry VI was free to receive visitors. According to

Warkworth's Chronicle, "every man was suffered [allowed] to come and speak with him, by licence of the keepers".[33]

In January 1466, Queen Elizabeth withdrew from public life to await the birth of her third child, accompanied by her ladies-in-waiting. Jacquetta, who was herself a mother of fourteen children, naturally took on the role of her daughter's mentor and offered her own valuable experience. It was Elizabeth's third delivery, so she knew what to expect in the birthing chamber, although she was still probably afraid of complications that so often carried young mothers to their early graves. The entire nation awaited the Queen's delivery with bated breath, expecting a male heir for the newly founded Yorkist dynasty. Dominic de Serigo, Edward IV's Italian physician, had assured the King "that the queen was conceived with a prince." When Elizabeth went into labour, the curious physician hovered outside the door, hoping to be the first to bring the happy news to the King. When, on 11 February 1466, the child cried, Master Dominic:

"[K]nocked or called secretly at the chamber door, and frayned [asked] what the Queen had. To whom it was answered by one of the ladies, 'Whatsoever the Queen's grace hath here within, sure it is that a fool stands there without,' and so confused with this answer, he departed without seeing of the King for that time."[34]

The Queen's first child by Edward was not a son, but a daughter who would be known to history as Elizabeth of York, mother of the Tudor dynasty. The baby girl was baptised on the day of her birth, with the Earl of Warwick, Jacquetta Woodville and Cecily, Duchess of York, acting as her godparents. Cecily's prominent role means she was reconciled with her son and his wife, at least outwardly. Around this time Cecily started using a new, more elaborate title, heading one of her letters as written "by the rightful inheritor's wife of the realm of England and of France, and lordship of Ireland, the King's mother, Duchess of York".[35] Cecily's insistence on using the title of "the rightful inheritor's wife" left no doubts as to how she perceived herself – she was the wife of a man who should have been King, so she, in theory, should have been Queen. Her husband's death robbed her of the chance to wear the crown, but she would make sure no one forgot about her rank and station. A herald account in later years made it clear that Cecily wasn't the only one who saw herself as a would-be royal consort, calling her a "Queen of right".[36]

Cecily manifestly did not appear at Elizabeth Woodville's churching ceremony, although it was one of the most spectacular celebrations of the newly established dynasty. Jacquetta was present during the churching held forty days after Elizabeth of York's birth and occupied a highly visible place in the procession and during the banquet. The churching procession and the banquet held afterwards were recorded by Bohemian visitors to Edward IV's court:

"The Queen left her child-bed that morning and went to church in stately order, accompanied by many priests bearing relics and by many scholars singing and carrying lights. There followed a great company of ladies and maidens from the country and from London, who had been summoned. Then came a great company of trumpeters, pipers and players of stringed instruments. The King's choir followed, forty-two of them, who sang excellently. Then came twenty-four heralds and pursuivants, followed by sixty counts and knights. At last came the Queen escorted by two dukes. Above her was a canopy. Behind her were her mother and maidens and ladies to the number of sixty. Then the Queen heard the singing of an Office, and, having left the church, she returned to her palace in procession as before. Then all who had joined the procession remained to eat. They sat down, women and men, ecclesiastical and lay, each according to rank, and filled four great rooms."[37]

Then the guests proceeded to "an unbelievably costly apartment where the Queen was preparing to eat". Lord Rozmital and his attendants were placed in an alcove so that they could observe this "great splendour". The Bohemian visitors were impressed not only with the solemnity of the ceremony itself but also with the huge amounts of exquisite food ("the food which was served to the Queen was most costly"), the respects paid to Elizabeth ("the courtly reverence paid to the Queen ... was such as I have never seen elsewhere") and the beauty of the Queen's ladies ("nor have I seen such exceedingly beautiful maidens"). King Edward IV made an impression as well: "We saw with what extraordinary reverence the King was treated by his servants. Even mighty counts had to kneel to him ... The King is a handsome, upstanding man and has the most splendid court that could be found in all Christendom."[38]

During the banquet, Jacquetta served her daughter, reversing the natural order according to which the daughters owed obedience and service to their parents:

"The Queen sat alone at table on a costly golden chair. The Queen's mother and the King's sister had to stand some distance away. When the Queen spoke with her mother or the King's sister, they knelt down before her until she had drunk water. Not until the first dish was set before the Queen could the Queen's mother and the King's sister be seated. The ladies and maidens and all who served the Queen at table were all of noble birth and had to kneel so long as the Queen was eating. The meal lasted for three hours . . . Everyone was silent and not a word was spoken."[39]

This lavish ceremony led some historians to assume that Elizabeth Woodville was a haughty queen who had forgotten about her humble origin. It is true that the banquet was very solemn and hardly a word was spoken during the three long hours while the Queen ate. It is true that Jacquetta "knelt before her", reversing the traditional role of daughterly obedience, and other ladies of high rank served her on bended knees as well. The occasion, however, called for celebration. Elizabeth had given birth to her first child by Edward IV, and although it was not the expected male heir, she had survived the labour and the child was Edward IV's first legitimate heir. Elizabeth's isolation from the rest of the court during the banquet—she sat alone at the table—was probably, as one historian pointed out, "conforming to queenly tradition".[40] Elizabeth featured so prominently during the banquet because Edward IV wanted to enhance his own regal status and present his Queen as the ideal consort and mother of his child.[41]

Jacquetta, now in her early fifties, would witness the births of two more royal granddaughters, Mary in August 1467 and Cecily (likely named after the King's mother) in March 1469, before her family would experience a dramatic turn of Fortune's Wheel.

NOTES

[1] Amy Licence, *Edward IV & Elizabeth Woodville: A True Romance*, p. 114.

[2] Dominic Mancini, *The Usurpation of Richard III*, p. 61.

[3] Conor Fahy, "The Marriage of Edward IV and Elizabeth Woodville: A New Italian Source", *The English Historical Review*, Vol. 76, No. 301 (Oct., 1961), pp. 660-672.

[4] Oliver Goldsmith, *History of England from the Invasion of Julius Caesar*, p. 143.

[5] Arlene Okerlund, *Elizabeth, England's Slandered Queen*, p. 17.

[6] Ibid., p. 24.

[7] Ibid., p. 15.

[8] David Baldwin, *Elizabeth Woodville: Mother of the Princes in the Tower*, p. 10.

[9] J. L. Laynesmith, *The Last Medieval Queens*, p. 66.

[10] Edward Hall, *Hall's Chronicle*, p. 264.

[11] *Calendar of State Papers and Manuscripts in the Archives and Collections of Milan 1385-1618*, n. 137.

[12] Arlene Okerlund, *Elizabeth Woodville, England's Slandered Queen*, p. 29.

[13] *Titulus Regius* http://www.richard111.com/titulus_regius.htm

14 Ibid.

15 Agnes Strickland, *Lives of the Queens of England*, Volume 3, p. 305.

16 Ibid.

17 As pointed out by Amy Licence in *Edward IV & Elizabeth Woodville: A True Romance*, p. 110.

18 *Calendar of State Papers and Manuscripts in the Archives and Collections of Milan 1385-1618*, n. 137.

19 Arlene Okerlund, *Elizabeth, England's Slandered Queen*, p. 60.

20 Gerard B. Wegemer and Travis Curtright (ed.), *The History of King Richard the Third*, p. 55.

21 Ibid.

22 Muriel St Clare Byrne (ed.), *The Lisle Letters*, Volume 1, p. 140.

23 Read more in Chapter 12.

24 Jennifer Scott, *The Royal Portrait: Image and Impact*, p. 26.

25 Arlene Okerlund, *Elizabeth, England's Slandered Queen*, p. 17.

26 Ibid., p. 15.

27 Sarah Gristwood, *Blood Sisters*, p. 84.

28 Antonia Gransden, *Historical Writing in England*, p. 271.

29 *Calendar of State Papers and Manuscripts in the Archives and Collections of Milan 1385-1618*, n. 142.

30 Ibid.

31 John Blacman, *Henry the Sixth*, p. 41.

32 Bertram Wolffe, *Henry VI*, p. 338.

33 *A Chronicle of the First Thirteen Years of the Reign of King Edward the Fourth*, by John Warkworth, p. 5.

34 Katharine N. Davies, *The First Queen Elizabeth*, p. 93.

35 Mary Anne Everett Wood, *Letters of Royal and Illustrious Ladies of Great Britain*, Volume 1, p. 106.

36 Caroline Amelia Halsted, *Richard III*, Volume 1, p. 442.

37 Malcolm Henry Ikin Letts, *The Travels of Leo of Rozmital*, p. 47.

38 Ibid., p. 5.

39 Ibid., p. 47.

40 Alfred Thomas, *A Blessed Shore: England and Bohemia from Chaucer to Shakespeare*, p. 163.

41 Ibid., p. 161.

CHAPTER 8:
"SLANDER OF WITCHCRAFT"

In 1469, a court jester told Edward IV that in some places the rivers were so high that he could scarce escape through them. He was referring to the fact that the Woodvilles (Jacquetta's husband was Lord Rivers) occupied prominent positions at court and their presence was highly visible.[1] Jacquetta's husband had become prominent in politics: in March 1466, he was appointed treasurer of England, he was created Earl Rivers on 25 May 1466, and he became Constable of England on 24 August 1467. Jacquetta attained the status of a great lady as attested by Margaret Paston's letter to her son John, wherein she asked him to try to arrange for one of his sisters "to be with my Lady of Oxford, or with my Lady of Bedford or in some other worshipful place whereas ye think best".[2] Despite her marriage to a social inferior, Jacquetta's rank as duchess was unchanged.

The Milanese ambassador reported that Jacquetta's royal daughter, "a widow of this island of quite low birth", did everything she could to honour her family:

"Since her coronation she has always exerted herself to aggrandise her relations, to wit, her father, mother, brothers and sisters. She had five brothers and as many sisters, and had brought things to such a pass that they had the entire government of this realm, to such an extent that the rest of the lords about the government were one, the Earl of Warwick, who has always been great and deservedly so."[3]

The aggrandisement of the Woodville family started in the mid-1460s and was achieved mostly through the marriages of Jacquetta's numerous children into the high ranks of the English nobility. The Woodvilles were soon linked to powerful noble families, and they were accused of obtaining the best possible matches. Jacquetta Woodville had five surviving sons, Anthony, Richard, John, Lionel and Edward, and seven daughters, Elizabeth, Jacquetta the younger, Anne, Mary, Margaret, Jane and Katherine. Some of them were married before Elizabeth Woodville became queen in 1464. Anthony was married to Elizabeth Scales, heiress of Thomas, Lord Scales. Jacquetta the younger was married to John Strange, Lord Strange of Knokyn. The rest of Jacquetta's children were unmarried, as were Elizabeth Woodville's two sons by John Grey.

The marrying of the Woodvilles started in the autumn of 1464, when Edward IV arranged a marriage between Margaret Woodville and Thomas FitzAlan, Baron Maltravers, the heir of the Earl of Arundel. On 17 February 1465, one John Wykes, a Paston correspondent, confirmed that the marriage went through since "the earl of Arundel's son hath wedded the Queen's sister".[4] More marriages followed: Anne married William Bourchier, the heir of the Earl of Essex, Joan married Anthony Grey, the eldest son of the Earl of Kent, Mary married William Herbert, Lord Dunster, the eldest son of William Herbert, Welsh baron – they were to become the Earl and Countess of Pembroke in 1466. One of the most scandalous marriages among Jacquetta's daughters occurred when her youngest, Katherine, born around 1458, married the Duke of Buckingham; she was already described as the duchess during Elizabeth's coronation, so it is possible that she married before May 1464. Katherine, aged around six at the time of Elizabeth's coronation, outranked all of her sisters save Elizabeth, attaining the title of duchess. One contemporary observer reported that the Duke of Buckingham "had been forced to marry the Queen's sister, whom he scorned to wed on account of her humble origin".[5]

While Jacquetta's daughters married in the 1460s, only one of her sons gained a wife in the aftermath of Elizabeth's coronation. John's match was to be the most scandalous of all because, at the age of twenty, he married the elderly Duchess of Norfolk, Edward IV's aunt (Cecily Neville's sister), who had already outlived three husbands and would, ironically, outlive her much younger spouse as well.[6] One of the contemporary chroniclers scornfully referred to the duchess as "a slip of a girl about eighty years old",[7] although she was about sixty at that time. Such an exaggeration served to point out the Woodville family's determination in achieving their goals; the marriage was deemed as "diabolical",[8] although there is no evidence that the elderly duchess was in any way forced to become John Woodville's wife.

Elizabeth Woodville's elder son, Jacquetta's grandson, Thomas Grey, Marquess of Dorset, married Edward IV's niece Anne Holland, whose hand in marriage had previously been promised to the Earl of Warwick's cousin George Neville. The Queen paid four thousand marks to Edward IV's sister, the Duchess of Exeter, for the marriage. These marriages outraged the Earl of Warwick, who resented the Woodvilles' influence. Katherine Woodville's marriage to the Duke of Buckingham caused "secret displeasure of the Earl of Warwick", and the match of Anne Holland and Thomas Grey caused Warwick "great and secret displeasure" since it was his brother who was jilted.[9]

Elizabeth Woodville naturally promoted the interests of her family, raising its members to familiarity with the King. She and her mother were seen as the representatives of the Woodville clan and became highly unpopular figures, at least where the Earl of Warwick was concerned. The nobles of the realm were as outraged at the rapid ennoblement of the Woodvilles as much as they were displeased with Edward IV's decision to marry a widow of low birth in utmost secrecy. All those factors combined together created a dangerous mixture of festering resentment that would eventually lead to an open rebellion against Edward IV.

In 1468, it was another marriage that would drive a wedge between Warwick and Edward IV. The King's sister Margaret was to marry Charles, who succeeded his father as Duke of Burgundy. It was a splendid match for Margaret of York and a lucrative political alliance for England, but Warwick was dissatisfied, as he promoted the French alliance. The Crowland chronicler explained:

"At this marriage, Richard Neville, earl of Warwick, who had for some years appeared to favour the party of the French against the Burgundians, conceived great indignation. For he would have greatly preferred to have sought an alliance for the said lady Margaret in the kingdom of France, by means of which, a favourable understanding might have arisen between the monarchs of those two kingdoms; it being much against his wish, that the views of Charles, now duke of Burgundy, should be in any way promoted by means of an alliance with England. The fact is, that he pursued that man with a most deadly hatred."[10]

The Woodville family was prominent during the festivities celebrating the marriage, and it was Anthony, Jacquetta's son, who presented Margaret of York at the Burgundian court. In the Crowland chronicler's view, it was Margaret of York's marriage to Duke Charles that enraged Warwick and strained the relations between him and Edward IV:

"This [marriage], in my opinion, was really the cause of the dissensions between the King and the earl, and not the one which has been previously mentioned — the marriage of the King with Queen Elizabeth. For this marriage of the King and Queen (although after some murmuring on the part of the earl, who had previously used his best endeavours to bring about an alliance between the king and the queen of Scotland, widow of the king of that country, lately deceased), had long before this been solemnly sanctioned and approved of at Reading, by the earl himself, and all the prelates and great lords of the kingdom. Indeed, it is the fact, that the earl continued to show favour to all the queen's kindred, until he found that her relatives and connexions, contrary to his wishes, were using their utmost endeavours to promote the other marriage, which, in conformity with the King's wishes, eventually took place between Charles and the lady Margaret, and were favouring other designs to which he was strongly opposed."[11]

This time Warwick would not forgive the slight. When Edward IV refused to grant royal licence for the marriage between his brother George, Duke of Clarence, and Warwick's eldest daughter, Isabel, Warwick snapped. Colluding with his brother, the Archbishop of Canterbury, Warwick applied for a papal dispensation for his daughter to marry Clarence and received it in March 1469. The couple were married on 11 July at Calais, with Cecily Neville, the groom's mother, waving them good-bye when they left the port at Sandwich.

Cecily's presence at Sandwich has been variously interpreted by historians, with some suggesting that she not only knew about Warwick's and Clarence's plans to rebel against Edward IV, but that she also gave them her blessing. Warwick now sought to remove Edward from the throne and replace him with his brother George. Warwick and Clarence claimed that Edward was illegitimate, reviving the story allegedly put forward by Cecily herself in 1464.[12] According to their story, Edward was the fruit of Cecily's extramarital affair. The implication was that since Edward was illegitimate, he was automatically unfit to rule. But how truthful was the claim of Edward's illegitimacy? Shortly before her death in 1495, Cecily herself denied the illegitimacy rumour, stating categorically in her last will that her late husband was the "father unto the most Christian Prince my Lord and son King Edward IV".[13] A rumour circulating in the courts of Burgundy and France later in Edward IV's reign had it that his real father was an archer called Blayborgne (or Blaybourne), hinting that Cecily had committed adultery.[14] Perhaps the 1469 accusation against Cecily was purely political and stemmed from what Cecily herself might have said to Edward IV upon discovering that he married Elizabeth Woodville. If so, she was partly responsible for the rumour and its implications.

On 12 July 1469, Warwick and Clarence, aided by the Archbishop of Canterbury, issued a manifesto lambasting Edward IV for relying too heavily on the counsel of his wife's family. They strongly condemned "the deceitful covetous rule and guiding of certain seditious persons, that is to say, the Lord Rivers, the Duchess of Bedford his wife, Sir William Herbert, Earl of Pembroke, Humphrey Stafford, Earl of Devonshire, the Lord Scales and Audley, Sir John Woodville and his brothers, Sir John Fogge, and others of their mischievous rule, opinion and assent, which have caused our said sovereign lord and his said realm to fall in great poverty of misery, disturbing the administration of the laws, only tending to their own promotion and enrichment".[15] Jacquetta's inclusion in this document proves just how influential she was with her daughter and the King.

On 26 July, Warwick and Clarence defeated Edward IV's army during the Battle of Edgecote Moor and took the King as their prisoner. England now had two captive kings, one languishing in the Tower, the other virtually imprisoned by his own cousin and brother. According to chronicler Jehan de Waurin, Warwick "greeted the King courteously without doing him any bodily harm" but decided to send him to the safety of his estate, Warwick

Castle, where Edward was "with guards, who led him every day to take exercise where he wished, to the limit of one league or two".[16]

Warwick's next step showed just how desperate—and dangerous—he had become. On 12 August 1469, he executed Richard Woodville, Earl Rivers, and his son John, who were captured after the Battle of Edgecote Moor. These executions were unlawful since Lord Rivers and his son had faithfully served Edward IV and had committed no treason against him. Their executions highlighted Warwick's frustration with Edward IV's regime and served his own personal vendetta. The tragic news reached London by 16 August, when the Milanese ambassador reported that "the Earl of Warwick, as astute a man as ever was Ulysses, is at the King's side, and from what they say the King is not at liberty to go where he wishes. The Queen is here and keeps very scant state".[17] According to chronicler Jehan de Waurin, Edward IV mourned the loss of his wife's father and brother "because he loved them very much".[18] Lord Rivers was posthumously described as the King's "true and faithful knight and liegeman", strongly suggesting that his loss was keenly felt.[19]

The executions of her beloved husband and son shocked Jacquetta, who would seek revenge on the perpetrators of this crime, but now she was in danger herself. Warwick, eager to annihilate the Woodvilles, used his allies to accuse Jacquetta of witchcraft. Jacquetta wasn't the first royal woman to be accused of witchcraft. In 1419, Joan of Navarre, widow of Henry IV, was arrested in her own manor at Havering-atte-Bower and accused of "compassing the death and destruction of our lord the King [Henry V] in the most treasonable and horrible manner that could be devised".[20] Her property was seized, and she was placed under house arrest. The contemporary chronicle recorded that she was allowed to retain nine ladies-in-waiting. Two account books of her household during a large portion of her captivity show that she lived in luxury and great comfort. On his deathbed in 1422, Henry V exonerated Joan, and she was soon released without suffering any harm.

Another woman who was accused of witchcraft during Jacquetta's lifetime was Joan of Arc, who was burned at the stake as a heretic on 30 May 1431. Jacquetta, whose relatives kept Joan under house arrest before she was handed over to the English, knew Joan's story well. Although Joan was burned as a heretic, an attempt was made to explain away the voices she claimed to hear as devilish sorcery. John, Duke of Bedford, Jacquetta's late husband, said of Joan that she was "a disciple and limb of the fiend that used false enchantments and sorcery".[21] Upon Joan's capture, the *Chronicle of London* recorded that she was "a false witch".[22] During Joan's trial she was persistently interrogated about the Fairy Tree that stood near her village of Domremy, where young women gathered during feast days and danced with garlands of flowers and herbs around their necks. Although Joan was burned as a heretic and schismatic, many believed her to have been a witch. Joan was posthumously exonerated in 1456 but was still remembered as sorceress in England. Chronicler Edward Hall, writing some hundred years after Joan's death, scathingly referred to her as "this witch or manly woman" who was "but an enchantress, an organ of the Devil, sent from Satan".[23]

In 1441, another royal woman was accused of dabbling in sorcery—her name was Eleanor, and she was Jacquetta's sister-in-law. The wife of Humphrey, Duke of Gloucester, Eleanor Cobham was a beautiful and ambitious woman who was well aware that if Henry VI died without male issue, her husband—or their children—would inherit the crown. Curious as to how long the young King would live, Eleanor asked her astrologer to cast the King's horoscope; he discovered that Henry VI would die of melancholia, a medieval term for depression, at the age of twenty. Imagining or predicting the death of a king was an act of treason in medieval England, and Eleanor's wish to discover how long Henry VI would live was later ascribed to her insatiable ambition to become Queen. Eleanor was also accused of employing Margery Jourdemayne, a local wise woman, to help her conceive a child. Margery was accused of supplying Eleanor with potions to induce the Duke of Gloucester to love and marry her. The implication was that since Gloucester had married Eleanor, Margery's witchcraft worked. Yet the case against Eleanor was not entirely baseless; she was interested in sorcery and astrology and admitted as much during her trial. Eventually Eleanor was found guilty by ecclesiastical law. She was divorced from Gloucester, stripped of her royal title, and ordered to perform a humiliating penitential walk through the crowded streets of London on three separate days. Eleanor never returned to the public sphere; she was sentenced to perpetual imprisonment at different locations until she died, disgraced and forgotten, at Beaumaris Castle, on 7 July 1452. Jacquetta may have witnessed Eleanor as she walked barefoot through the streets of London "with a meek and demure countenance", carrying a two-pound lighted candle that she later offered at the altar at Westminster Abbey.[24]

With these examples still vivid in her memory, Jacquetta was terrified when she was arrested and brought to Warwick Castle, where Edward IV was held captive. Her chief accuser, Thomas Wake, was loyal to the Earl of Warwick, and brought a lead image "made like a man of arms . . . broken in the middle and made fast with a wire, saying that it was made by her to use with witchcraft and sorcery". He also claimed that a parish clerk from Northampton, John Daunger, could testify that Jacquetta had fashioned two more images, one representing Edward IV and the other representing the Queen, her own daughter.[25] It was never explained what purpose these images served, although the implication was that Jacquetta used love magic to bring Edward IV and her daughter Elizabeth together, as was rumoured after their marriage. In 1483, Richard III's Parliament suggested as much when the case against Jacquetta was revived, including also her daughter Elizabeth:

"And here also we consider, how that the said pretended marriage betwixt the above-named king Edward and Elizabeth Grey, was made of great presumption, without the knowledge and assent of the lords of this land, and also by sorcery and witchcraft committed by the said Elizabeth, and her mother Jacquetta, duchess of Bedford, as the common opinion of the people, and the public voice and fame is throughout all this land, and hereafter, if the cause shall require, shall be proved sufficiently in time and place convenient."[26]

Modern readers will probably remember that Jacquetta and Elizabeth Woodville are depicted as sorceresses in Philippa Gregory's bestselling novels, *The Lady of The Rivers* and *The White Queen,* and in a television show based on the novels. Philippa Gregory incorporated the legend of mythical water goddess Melusine into her novel because Elizabeth Woodville was said to have claimed descent from Melusine through Jacquetta.

The tale of Melusine, a mythical creature portrayed in legends and folklore as a serpent or fish from the waist down—similar to a mermaid—was known as one of the many "ancestral romances". *The Romance of Melusine,* written in 1393 in France, gained astonishing popularity. Written by Jean of Arras, *The Romance of Melusine* was a work of fiction commissioned to address certain political controversy.[27] This medieval novel became so tremendously successful that it soon appeared in England, Spain and Germany. Jacquetta Woodville owned a copy of *The Romance of Melusine,*[28] probably because it was an international bestseller and, as historian Nancy Goldstone pointed out, "it was almost impossible for a literate person not to be aware of this book".[29] We do not know, however, if Jacquetta or Elizabeth were especially interested in the legend of Melusine, and as J. L. Laynesmith pointed out, there is no "explicit association between Elizabeth Woodville and her legendary ancestor in surviving documents".[30]

It is often assumed by historians that the 1469 case against Jacquetta eventually collapsed when Warwick's rebellion failed and Edward was released from captivity, but the late historian John Ashdown Hill suggested that Jacquetta was found guilty because this verdict would explain why she was so eager to clear her name from slander later on. According to Ashdown Hill:

"It is, of course, true that we have no surviving record of the proceedings initially undertaken against Jacquette [sic] by Warwick and Clarence. However, it is almost as certain that they would have had her found guilty as that Edward IV (once he was at liberty) would ensure that she was declared innocent. In fact, Jacquette's concern to have herself exonerated by her son-in-law strongly suggests that she had previously been judged guilty by those employed by Warwick and Clarence."[31]

Whether she was found guilty or not, Jacquetta would never forget the slight. In January 1470, she went before the King's great council, where she accused Thomas Wake of being of a "malicious disposition" toward her "of long time continued, intending not only to hurt and impair her good name and fame, but also purposing the final destruction of her person".[32] The wording of Jacquetta's complaint clearly shows that she believed she was in mortal danger at the time. Naturally, she denied the charges and proclaimed that she had always "truly believed in God according to the faith of Holy Church, as a true Christian Woman ought to do".[33] Her accusers withdrew their statements:

"Thomas Wake says that this image was shown and left in Stoke with an honest person who delivered it to the clerk of the church and so showed it to divers neighbours after to the parson in the church openly to men both of Shetyllanger and Stoke and after it was shown in Sewrisley, a nunnery, and to many other persons, and of all this he heard or wist nothing till after it was sent him by Thomas Kymbell from the said clerk. John Daunger of Shetyllanger said that Thomas Wake sent to him one Thomas Kymbell, then his bailiff, and bad the said John send him the image of lead that he had and so he sent it, at which time he heard no witchcraft of the lady of Bedford, and that the image was delivered to him by one Harry Kyngeston of Stoke, who found it in his house after the departing of soldiers, and that the said Thomas Wake after he came from London from the king sent for him and said that he had excused himself and laid all the blame on John and bad him say that he durst not keep the image and for that cause sent it to Thomas and also bad him say that there were two other images, one for the king and one for the queen, but he refused to say so."[34]

Bizarrely, the Earl of Warwick, the man who engineered the case against her, was present when Jacquetta was proclaimed innocent. Unfortunately for Jacquetta and her daughter, Edward IV decided to forgive Warwick and Clarence.

NOTES

1 "The Ryvers been soo hie", cited in J. Laynesmith, *The Last Medieval Queens*, p. 200.
2 J. Fenn, A. Ramsed (ed.), *Paston Letters: Original Letters Written During the Reigns of Henry VI*, p. 195, p. 17.
3 *Calendar of State Papers, Milan: 1469*, n. 173.
4 J. Fenn, A. Ramsed (ed.), *Paston Letters: Original Letters Written During the Reigns of Henry VI*, p. 195.
5 Dominic Mancini, *The Usurpation of Richard III*, p. 75.
6 Arlene Okerlund, *Elizabeth, England's Slandered Queen*, p. 78.
7 Keith Dockray, *Edward IV: A Sourcebook*, p. 48.
8 Ibid.
9 Susan Higginbotham, *The Woodvilles*, p. 35.

[10] *The Crowland Chronicle: Part IV*, http://www.r3.org/on-line-library-text-essays/crowland-chronicle/part-v/

[11] Ibid.

[12] Read more in Chapter 7.

[13] John Gough Nichols, *Wills from Doctors' Commons*, p. 1.

[14] Livia Visser-Fuchs, Review of Michael K. Jones's *Bosworth 1485. Psychology of a Battle* in *The Ricardian: Journal of the Richard III Society*, Volume 14, p. 3.

[15] A. R. Myers (ed.), *English historical documents. 4. [Late medieval]. 1327 - 1485*, p. 295.

[16] Ibid., p. 297.

[17] *Calendar of State Papers, Milan: 1469*, n. 173.

[18] Jehan de Waurin, *Recueil des Chroniques et Anchiennes Histories de la Grant Bretaigne*, Volume 5, p. 581.

[19] *Rotuli Parliamentorum*, Volume VI, p. 232.

[20] A.R. Myers, *The Captivity of a Royal Witch: The Household Accounts of Queen Joan of Navarre, 1419-21*, p. 264.

[21] L. Mahon, *Joan of Arc*, p. 71.

[22] George Townsend Warner, (ed.), *English History Illustrated From Original Sources: 1399-1485*, Volume 3, p. 87.

[23] Edward Hall, *Hall's Chronicle*, p. 157.

[24] *An English Chronicle of the Reigns of Richard II, Henry IV, Henry V, and Henry VI*, p. 59.

[25] *CPR, Edward IV, Henry VI, 1467-1477*, p. 190.

[26] Rapin de Thoyras, *The History of England*, Volume 12, p. 278.

[27] Nancy Goldstone, *The Maid and the Queen*, p. 14.

[28] Luxembourg, Jaquetta de, Duchess of Bedford and Countess Rivers (c.1416–1472), Noblewoman by Lucia Diaz Pascual, Oxford Dictionary of National Biography. http://www.oxforddnb.com/view/printable/101258

[29] Nancy Goldstone, *The Maid and the Queen*, p. 14.

[30] J. L. Laynesmith, *The Last Medieval Queens*, p. 40.

[31] John Ashdown Hill, *The Third Plantagenet: George, Duke of Clarence, Richard III's Brother* (Kindle edition).

[32] *CPR, Edward IV, Henry VI, 1467-1477*, p. 190.

[33] *Rotuli Parliamentorum*, Volume VI, p. 232.

[34] *CPR, Edward IV, Henry VI, 1467-1477*, p. 190.

CHAPTER 9:
RETURN OF THE QUEEN

Edward IV's decision to extend his royal pardon towards Warwick and Clarence was one of his weakest political courses of action, motivated, no doubt, by feelings of family obligation. Although following his release from captivity, the King reportedly had "good language of the lords of Clarence [and] of Warwick . . . saying that they be his best friends", his court was seething with anger. One of the Paston correspondents recorded the King's "household men have other language, so what shall hastily fall I cannot see".[1]

In March 1470, Cecily of York invited her two sons to her home at Baynard's Castle, but shortly afterward Warwick and Clarence rebelled yet again, this time taking their grievances overseas. They did the unthinkable and reached out to Margaret of Anjou, the Lancastrian queen in exile.

By 1470, Margaret was residing with her son at her father's court in the duchy of Bar. Her uncle and ally Charles VII of France died in July 1461 and his successor, Louis XI, was unwilling to invest his time and resources into helping

Margaret reinstate her husband onto the throne. This changed when Warwick reached out to Louis asking him if he would intercede on his behalf with Margaret and propose a truce. Margaret and Prince Edward arrived at the castle of Amboise on 25 June 1470, where they were "received in a very friendly and honourable manner" by Louis XI and his wife, Charlotte of Savoy.[2]

The French King spent several days "in long discussions" with Margaret, who entertained doubts about Warwick's change of heart. Deep down she must have wondered whether his change of loyalties was not just a ruse to lure her back to England and straight into prison. "Up to the present the Queen has shown herself very hard and difficult, and although his Majesty offers her many assurances, it seems that on no account whatever will she agree to send her son with Warwick, as she mistrusts him", wrote the Milanese ambassador at the French court.[3] To convince the Queen of the sincerity of his plans, Warwick proposed a marriage alliance between Margaret's son, Prince Edward, and his younger daughter, Anne Neville. By 20 July, Margaret "has been induced to consent to do all that his Majesty desires, both as regards reconciliation with Warwick and the marriage alliance".[4] Still, she was unwilling to allow her son to join Warwick's expedition and decided that the prince would stay with her and join Warwick in England if the earl's enterprise was successful.

On 22 July 1470, Margaret met the Earl of Warwick and his family at Angers Cathedral. She now stood face-to-face with the man who had besmirched her reputation, cast slanders on her son's paternity and was responsible for Henry VI's deposition in 1461. "With great reverence Warwick went on his knees and asked her pardon for the injuries and wrongs done to her in the past", wrote the ambassador who observed the scene. Margaret kept Warwick on his knees for several minutes before she "graciously forgave him". The whole spectacle was carefully arranged by Louis XI, who was present in the cathedral when Warwick "did homage and fealty there, swearing to be a faithful and loyal subject of the king, queen and prince as his liege lords unto death".[5]

By 28 July 1470, the marriage between Prince Edward and Anne Neville was solemnly announced at the French court. Warwick was eager for the marriage to be consummated immediately to ensure that it was indissoluble in the eyes of God. But there was a delay, as it transpired that Edward and Anne were related in the fourth degree of consanguinity, and the pope's dispensation was deemed necessary to ensure that the match was lawful. It took five months for the pope to issue the desired dispensation, and the young couple was married on 13 December 1470 at the castle of Amboise.

Warwick was not there for his daughter's nuptials, as he had left France at the head of an army in September 1470. On 3 October, Sir Geoffrey Gate, Warwick's agent, secured the surrender of the Tower of London. On 5 October, Archbishop Neville entered the City of London and installed a new garrison loyal to his brother, the earl. Then Warwick himself "went to the Tower of London where King Harry was in prison by King Edward's commandment, and there took him from his keepers, which was not worshipfully arrayed as a prince, and not so cleanly kept as should seem such a prince".[6]

It was a sudden change of regime. Edward IV fled the country to seek aid at the court of his sister in Burgundy. At this point, the Yorks were defeated, or so it appeared. Queen Elizabeth Woodville was terrified of what would happen to her and her loved ones now that they were at the mercy of the victorious Lancastrians. She knew that Warwick blamed her and her family for the loss of his influence, as was painfully evidenced when he executed her father and brother in 1469. Jacquetta, who had recently been accused of witchcraft by Warwick's men, must have also feared for her own safety. Both women decided to seek sanctuary at Westminster Abbey. Writing on 12 October 1470, John Paston informed his mother that "the Queen that was, and the Duchess of Bedford, be in sanctuary at Westminster".[7] It is remarkable that Elizabeth was referred to as "the Queen that was", as if her husband's nine-year reign was just an insignificant interlude between Henry VI's deposition and restoration.

Although sanctuary offered security, Elizabeth and Jacquetta feared that its walls could be breached. On 3rd October, the Queen begged the mayor and aldermen of London to take charge of the Tower and keep the city against the Kentishmen, who had assembled at Southwark in support of the Earl of Warwick and began their pillage in the suburbs. Elizabeth feared that "the said Kentishmen and others would invade the said sanctuary of Westminster to despoil and kill" her.[8] The "others" were certainly Warwick and Clarence, whom the Woodville women perceived as enemies of their family.

It is sometimes asserted that Jacquetta, her daughter and three little granddaughters were cooped up together in uncomfortable conditions in the sanctuary, but this is far from the truth. The medieval house of the abbots of

Westminster was known as Cheyneygates and dated back to the fourteenth century. One of the most sumptuous parts of this place was the spacious Jerusalem Chamber, with its walls covered with rich tapestries—it was in this chamber where King Henry IV died in 1413. Although she was no longer Queen, Elizabeth didn't lack for basic needs and was provided with "half a beef and two muttons" a week for her table by William Gould, London butcher.

Henry VI knew that Warwick had a brutal streak and made sure that people who sought sanctuary were treated with respect. As a religious man, Henry found the idea of violating the safety of a holy place repellent and decreed that anyone who sought sanctuary should not be driven out by force. He graciously allowed Elizabeth Woodville's trusted midwife, Margery Cobbe, and Dr Serigo to join her at Westminster and appointed Elizabeth, Baroness Scrope of Bolton, to serve her. Elizabeth gave birth to the long-awaited son, Prince Edward, on 2 November 1470 within the confines of Cheyneygates. Some sources state that Lady Scrope acted as the child's godmother, but it seems more likely that Jacquetta was picked for this honour or that the two women stood as godmothers together.

On 19 December 1470, Margaret of Anjou, accompanied by Warwick's wife, Prince Edward and Anne Neville, took her leave of Louis XI. The Milanese ambassador incorrectly reported that they returned to England; in fact, Margaret's departure was delayed until April 1471 by unfavourable winds. In March 1471, Edward IV returned from exile with an army of seven thousand men. As he marched towards London, he "sent comfortable messages to the Queen at Westminster". Edward entered the City on 11 April. Edward used his charms to attract as many supporters as he could. Many people preferred this young, athletic and valiant man to Henry VI, whom they perceived as a puppet in Warwick's hands. Philippe de Commines, a writer and diplomat in the courts of Burgundy and France, observed that Edward was so warmly received because of the "great debts he owed in the city, which made his merchant creditors support him" and because "several noblewomen and wives of the rich citizens with whom he had been closely and secretly acquainted won over their husbands and relatives to his cause".[9]

Edward stopped by St Paul's Cathedral to offer thanks for his unopposed entry to London and to secure the person of Henry VI. The Lancastrian King resided in the Bishop's Palace, a little distance southeast from the cathedral, where Edward came to see him. Henry displayed a calm countenance when he saw Edward, embraced his rival and surrendered, saying: "My cousin of York, you are very welcome. I know that in your hands I will not be in danger."[10] Edward sent Henry to the Tower once again, and Henry appeared to have been glad at such a turn of events. Perhaps he was just tired of fighting for the crown and wished to retire from public and live the quiet life of a royal recluse. Even so, it is stunning that he relinquished his claim so easily and didn't take a more decisive stance against Edward. It's possible that by surrendering, Henry sought to avoid bloodshed and hoped that Edward would not punish Margaret of Anjou and Prince Edward of Westminster, who still didn't know what was happening in England.

After securing Henry VI's person, Edward IV headed directly to Westminster Abbey, where he "made his devout prayers and gave thanks to God, St Peter and St Edward". After prayers, the King went to see his wife and their children at the sanctuary. Jacquetta, who was still with her daughter, witnessed a tearful family reunion. Edward was moved when his Queen showed him their first son, Prince Edward, born five months earlier. The newly reunited royal family travelled a short distance from Westminster Abbey to Baynard's Castle, the London residence of the King's mother, Cecily, Duchess of York, "where they heard divine service that night".[11] It appears that any animosities that previously existed between Cecily and the Woodville women were now gone.

But the war was not over yet, for Warwick was marching towards London with his army, ready to fight for the Lancastrian cause. Henry VI may have surrendered, but he still had a son and heir who had been groomed to challenge Edward IV's claim. Jacquetta, her daughter and grandchildren were moved to the safety of the Tower, uncertain if Edward would emerge victorious. Cecily joined them, but she worked tirelessly behind the scenes to convince her wayward son George of Clarence to switch sides and join Edward IV against Warwick.[12]

George rebelled with Warwick twice. Edward forgave them their first trespass, but he would not do so the second time. If George met Edward in the open field, he would either die in battle or be taken prisoner and face imminent execution. When George first rebelled against Edward, he hoped that Warwick would place him on the throne. It made sense then, as Edward didn't have a male heir yet. Now, with Warwick's daughter married to Henry VI's son, George's chance to ever become king was slight.

Still, he made a secret pact with Margaret of Anjou that if her son died childless, George would be the next king.[13] Yet he must have understood that such a scenario was highly unlikely, for her son was young and married to Anne Neville, and there was every reason to expect a child of this union. George probably saw how futile it was to place his hopes with the Lancastrians, and when his mother and sisters were using "right covert ways and means" to heal the rift between the York brothers, George decided to switch sides yet again and joined his family, leaving Warwick and Margaret of Anjou to fend for themselves.[14]

The armies of Warwick and Edward IV met at Barnet on 14 April 1471, where Edward won the day. Warwick was slain on the battlefield, as was his brother, Lord Montague. Jacquetta Woodville's son Anthony and the King's youngest brother, Richard of Gloucester, were said to have been "severely wounded, but they had no harm from it, God be praised".[15] Edward IV took Warwick's and Montague's bodies to London and displayed them publicly at St Paul's Cathedral to show to the people that the rebels and traitors were dead. In an age of no newspapers, the only way to prove a person's death was to display the body publicly. For three days, Warwick's corpse was placed on display "open and naked", except for a cloth to cover his privy parts, to quash the rumours that he was still alive.[16]

Margaret of Anjou, her son and their allies landed at Weymouth on the same day the Battle of Barnet took place. When Margaret learned of Warwick's defeat, she was "right heavy and sorry" but far from defeated. Warwick was her ally, but Margaret never trusted him completely, and she still hoped her army would be able to crush Edward IV and restore her husband to the throne. It's possible that as Margaret marched north through Exeter, Taunton, Glastonbury, Wells and Bath, she was already thinking about orchestrating Henry VI's abdication and placing her son on the throne.

Prince Edward of Westminster was far from a feeble figurehead, as his father had always been. He spent his childhood as a fugitive, but Margaret made sure that her son never forgot about his destiny. In 1467, when he was thirteen years old, he was said to have talked "of nothing but of cutting off heads or making war, as if he had everything in his hands or was the god of battle or the peaceful occupant of that throne".[17] This short description defined Edward of Westminster's historical reputation, for he is often portrayed as a violent and cruel young man, both in nonfiction and novels. But what this short report proves is rather that the young Lancastrian prince was groomed to challenge Edward IV's claim to England's throne. John Fortescue, Chief Justice of the King's Bench and the author of *Commendation of the Laws of England,* painted a picture of a military-oriented young prince eager to reclaim his birthright:

"The prince, as soon as he became grown up, gave himself over entirely to martial exercises; and, seated on fierce and half-tamed steeds urged on by his spurs, he often delighted in attacking and assaulting the young companions attending him, sometimes with a lance, sometimes with a sword, sometimes with other weapons, in a warlike manner and in accordance with the rules of military discipline."[18]

From his childhood, Edward of Westminster was told that he was "going to be king", and he assumed an air of authority and delighted in military exercises, trying to emulate his grandfather Henry V. Appointed as Lieutenant of the Realm of England, upon his landing at Weymouth Edward of Westminster sent letters to potential allies, calling them to take up arms against Edward IV, whom he described as "Edward Earl of March, the King's great rebel, our enemy".[19]

On 4 May 1471, Margaret of Anjou's army arrived at Tewkesbury. According to one contemporary chronicle, the Queen didn't take part in the fighting, but took shelter at "a poor religious house whither she had fled for safety of her life".[20] Chronicler Edward Hall, however, asserted that Margaret took on a more active role:

"The Queen and her son prince Edward rode about the field, encouraging their soldiers, promising them (if they did show themselves valiant against their enemies) great rewards and high promotions, innumerable gain of the spoil and booty of their adversaries, and above all other fame and renown throughout the whole realm."[21]

Prince Edward of Westminster was in nominal command of the centre of the army, aided by John, Lord Wenlock, and John Langstrother, Prior of St John. Despite all his valour and military skill, the Lancastrian prince was killed. There are multiple, often contradictory, accounts of his death. According to the Yorkist *History of the Arrival of Edward IV,* "Edward, called Prince, was taken, fleeing to the town wards, and slain in the field".[22] *Wakworth's Chronicle* asserted that he was killed "in the field" and "cried for succour to his brother-in-law, the Duke of Clarence".[23] A Norwich register for 1470-71 states curiously that Edward of Westminster was not killed in the battle but tried before a military tribunal and summarily executed afterwards.[24] In 1473, it was claimed that the Lancastrian prince was struck in the face by Edward IV and murdered in his presence. It is not entirely inconceivable that Edward IV met with Edward of Westminster, either on the battlefield or afterwards. Writing on 2 June 1471, Sforza di Bettini of Florence, Milanese Ambassador in France, asserted that:

"Yesterday his Majesty here [Louis XI] heard with extreme sorrow, by clear and manifest news from England, so it appears, that king Edward has recently fought a battle with the Prince of Wales, towards Wales, whither he had gone to meet him. He has not only routed the prince but taken and slain him, together with all the leading men with him."[25]

According to the *Great Chronicle of London*:

"The king assembled his people and drew towards his enemies and finally met with them at a place or village called Tewkesbury, where after a short fight he subdued his enemies and took Queen Margaret and her son alive. The which being brought into his presence, after the king had questioned a few words of the cause of his so landing within his realm, and he gave unto the king an answer contrary to his pleasure, the king smote him on the face with the back of his gauntlet. After which stroke so received by him, the king's servants rid him out of life forthwith."[26]

Putting together the bits and pieces he heard over the course of writing his book, Polydore Vergil, in the sixteenth century, claimed that Edward of Westminster was brought before Edward IV, who struck him when the youth boldly stated that he had come to England to claim his birthright. Then, Vergil states, Edward of Westminster was "cruelly murdered" in the King's presence by George, Duke of Clarence, Richard, Duke of Gloucester and William, Lord Hastings.[27] Whatever the truth behind the manner of his death, Edward of Westminster lost his life on 4 May 1471. Margaret of Anjou was nowhere near the battlefield, taking refuge in a "poor religious place". By 7 May, she was found, accompanied by Anne Neville, widowed Princess of Wales, Marie Courtenay, Countess of Devon, and Katherine Vaux. The women were taken to London, Margaret travelling in a carriage and displayed as a trophy of war.

Anthony Woodville, Jacquetta's son, was not with the King at Tewkesbury. He stayed behind in London to defend the capital from the attack of the Bastard of Fauconberg, the illegitimate son of William Neville, Lord Fauconberg. The *Crowland Chronicle* praised Anthony for saving the Londoners:

"[I]t was not God's will that such a famous city, the capital indeed of the whole realm of England, should be given over to pillage by such great rogues. He gave stout hearts to the Londoners to enable them to stand firm on the day of battle. In this they were especially assisted by a sudden and unexpected sortie from the Tower of London by Anthony, Earl Rivers. As the enemy were making fierce assaults on the gate [...] he fell upon their rear with his mounted troops and gave the Londoners the opportunity to open their gates and fight it out hand to hand with the enemy so that they manfully put each and every one of them to death or to flight."[28]

Edward IV returned triumphantly to London on 21 May 1471. One of his first decisions was to lock Margaret of Anjou in the Tower, but it's unlikely she was placed in the same suite as her husband, Henry VI, who died that same day. There are various accounts of his death. Writing on 17 June, the Milanese ambassador at the French court asserted that Edward IV "has caused King Henry to be secretly assassinated in the Tower, where he was a prisoner. They say he has done the same to the Queen, King Henry's wife. He has, in short, chosen to crush the seed".[29] Margaret was still alive, but rumours spread that Henry VI died a violent death.

Warkworth's Chronicle states that Henry VI had been "put to death, the twenty-first day of May, on a Tuesday night, between eleven and twelve of the clock, being then at the Tower the Duke of Gloucester, brother to the King Edward and many other". Fabyan's Chronicle claimed that "the most common fame went that he [Henry VI] was stikked [stabbed] with a dagger by the hands of Richard of Gloucester". Philippe de Commines also wrote that "if what was told me be true . . . the Duke of Gloucester slew this poor King Henry with his own hand, or caused him to be carried into some private place, and stood by while he was killed". The only contemporary source claiming that Henry VI wasn't murdered is the Yorkist *History of the Arrival of Edward IV*, stating that Henry VI died "of pure displeasure and melancholy" upon hearing the news about the defeat of his armies and his son's death. It's not inconceivable that Henry VI died of a heart attack upon receiving the devastating news, but a source lauding Edward IV as a hero is not the most reliable of documents since it sought to depict Edward in the most favourable terms. At the exhumation of Henry's remains in 1910, evidence was found—hair apparently matted with blood—which suggested that he met his death by violence. According to tradition still passed down during the tours in the Tower of

London, Henry died at Wakefield Tower, where he was murdered as he knelt at prayer. If it's true, he died as he lived: piously, with a prayer on his lips.

NOTES

[1] J. Fenn, A. Ramsed (ed.), *Paston Letters: Original Letters Written During the Reigns of Henry VI*, Volume 1, p. 195, p. 7.

[2] *Calendar of State Papers and Manuscripts in the Archives and Collections of Milan 1385-1618*, n. 189.

[3] Ibid.

[4] Ibid., n. 190.

[5] Ibid, n. 191.

[6] Jeffrey James, *Edward IV: Glorious Son of York*, p. 58.

[7] J. Fenn, A. Ramsed (ed.), *Paston Letters: Original Letters Written During the Reigns of Henry VI, Edward IV and Richard III*, Two Volumes in One, p. 53.

[8] Reginald R Sharpe, *London And The Kingdom*, Volume 3, p. 386.

[9] Arlene Okerlund, *Elizabeth: England's Slandered Queen*, p. 126.

[10] Betram Wolffe, *Henry VI*, p. 345.

[11] John Allen Giles, *The Chronicles of the White Rose of York: A Series of Historical Fragments*, p. 61.

[12] Monique Sommé, *La Correspondance d'Isabelle de Portugal, Duchesse de Bourgogne (1430-1471)*, p. 343.

[13] This is clearly stated in the articles against George when he committed treason in 1478.

[14] *The Historie of the Arrival of King Edward IV:* http://www.r3.org/on-line-library-text-essays/the-arrivall-of-edward-iv/part-ii-landing-through-the-reconciliation-with-clarence/

[15] Hannes Kleineke, 'Gerhard von Wesel's Newsletter from England, 17 April 1471', *The Ricardian*, 16 (2006), p. 81.

[16] *The Historie of the Arrival of King Edward IV*, op.cit.

[17] *Calendar of State Papers and Manuscripts in the Archives and Collections of Milan 1385-1618*, n. 146.

[18] John Fortescue, *De Laudibus Legum Anglie*, p. 3.

[19] Letter to John Daunt quoted in P. W. Hammond, *The Battles of Barnet and Tewkesbury*, p. 81.

[20] John Allen Giles, *The Chronicles of the White Rose of York*, p. 76.

[21] Edward Hall, *Hall's Chronicle*, p. 300.

22 Keith Dockray, *A sourcebook*, p. 133.
23 Ibid.
24 James E. Thorold Rogers, *A History of Agriculture and Prices in England*, p. 713 n. 1.
25 *Calendar of State Papers and Manuscripts in the Archives and Collections of Milan 1385-1618*, n. 218.
26 Alec Reginald Myers, David Charles Douglas (ed.), *English Historical Documents. 4. [Late medieval]. 1327 - 1485*, p. 310.
27 *Works of the Camden Society*, Volume 29, p. 152.
28 *Crowland*, p. 129.
29 *Calendar of State Papers and Manuscripts in the Archives and Collections of Milan 1385-1618*, n. 220.

CHAPTER 10: WON AND LOST CAUSES

On 26 June 1471, Edward IV made his son Prince of Wales and later that year appointed a fifteen-member council for his infant son, of which Queen Elizabeth and her brother Anthony Woodville were members. Jacquetta, the indomitable Duchess of Bedford, proudly observed as her two eldest children received recognition for their efforts during the past months. The poem entitled "On the Recovery of the Throne by Edward IV" sang praises to Queen Elizabeth and Anthony, who now carried his late father's title of Earl Rivers. Elizabeth was praised as a "blessed creature" who endured much "languor and anguish" when "her lord and sovereign was in adversity". "To hear of her weeping it was great pity", the poem said, giving us a rare insight into the troubled minds of Elizabeth and her mother during that difficult time.[1] Anthony, "that gentle knight", was also praised for his part in saving the Queen and the city of London from the Bastard of Fauconberg's assault. "Blessed be the time that he born was" was also a nod of approval to Jacquetta, acknowledging her as the mother of the new national hero.[2]

The royal family spent Christmas of 1471 at the Palace of Westminster, keeping an open household and awing spectators with public displays of royal magnificence. Much like King Stephen in the twelfth century, Edward IV used his Christmas court to impress his status and authority on the people of England. After his release from captivity in 1141, King Stephen was re-crowned by Archbishop Theobald. Following this precedent, Edward IV ceremoniously wore his crown:

"On Christmas Day the King our sovereign lord, Edward IV after the conquest, was crowned at Westminster, and the Queen also. He kept his estate in the White Hall the same day. The Bishop of Rochester, who sang mass the same day of coronation, sat at the King's board on the right hand, and the Duke of Buckingham on the left hand."[3]

This was something more than just a crown-wearing ceremony: it was a reminder that Edward IV was still King of England and that the house of Lancaster was defeated. On New Year's Day, "the King and Queen went in procession" without wearing their crowns. On Twelfth Day, yet another procession showed Edward IV wearing his crown, but Elizabeth was "not crowned because she was great with child".[4]

It was a new dawn for the Yorks. Yet the shadows of the past were still lingering on, refusing to be forgotten. Margaret of Anjou, locked in the Tower, was soon moved to Windsor Castle. On 8 January 1472, John Paston wrote that the former queen was "removed from Windsor to Wallingford, nigh to Ewelme, my Lady of Suffolk's place in Oxfordshire".[5] Alice, Dowager Duchess of Suffolk, was the widow of William de la Pole, who had negotiated Margaret's marriage to Henry VI and who had been appointed by the King to bring her to England so many years ago. The duchess's only son, John, was constable of Wallingford Castle and, more importantly, husband of Edward IV's sister Elizabeth, Duchess of Suffolk.

On 17 February 1472, John Paston wrote:

"Yesterday the King, the Queen, my lords of Clarence and Gloucester, went to Sheen to pardon, men say not all in charity. What will fall men cannot say. The King entertained my lord of Clarence for my lord of Gloucester, and it is said he answered that he may well have my lady his sister-in-law, but they shall part no livelihood, as he said; so what will fall I cannot say."[6]

This meeting at Sheen highlighted the tensions within the royal family. In the aftermath of Tewkesbury,

Edward IV's youngest brother, Richard, Duke of Gloucester, decided to marry Anne Neville, daughter of the late Earl of Warwick and widow of Edward of Westminster. The two knew each other well, for Richard spent his boyhood years in the Neville household at Middleham Castle. Following her husband's death, Anne submitted to Edward IV and was placed under the custody of her elder sister, Isabel, and her husband, George, Duke of Clarence.

Anne's life couldn't have been easy. Her late father died fighting for Henry VI's cause, and her husband was the last Lancastrian heir. Her troublesome brother-in-law, who betrayed her father's trust, now sought to appropriate her part of the Warwick inheritance as well. Knowing that Richard wanted to marry Anne, George sent her disguised as a kitchen maid to sanctuary at St Martin's, but Richard found Anne and asked Edward IV's permission to marry her.[7] The King agreed and stipulated that the Warwick inheritance should be divided between the two sisters and their husbands. Missing from the equation was the girls' mother, Anne Beauchamp, Countess of Warwick, who fled to sanctuary following her husband's defeat at Barnet.

When Clarence deserted Warwick and re-joined his royal brother, the two were reconciled, largely due to the efforts of their mother and sisters. Clarence's offences were forgotten. As reward for his defection and services at Barnet, Clarence had immediately been granted all the Warwick inheritance which his wife Isabel had been entitled to inherit. George and Isabel wanted to keep Isabel's inheritance, but there was one problem: Warwick's widow, mother of the Neville sisters, was still alive. She could expect no dower from her late husband's estates since, in Edward IV's eyes, Warwick had been a traitor. Anne, Countess of Warwick, was still entitled to her jointure, the impressive portfolio of lands and properties settled jointly on her and her husband at their marriage. Moreover, she had inherited the Despenser and Beauchamp lands from her father, and these legally belonged to her.

Unable to leave sanctuary, the countess was virtually a prisoner. Immured at Beaulieu, she wrote desperate pleas "to the right worshipful and discreet commons of this present Parliament", begging them to look favourably upon her plea. The widowed countess was well aware that many powerful women close to the King could help her, and so she directed her:

"[L]abours, suits, and means to the King's Highness, soothly also to the Queen's good grace, to my right redoubted lady the King's mother [Cecily, Duchess of York], to my lady the King's eldest daughter [Elizabeth of York], to my lords the King's brethren, to my ladies the King's sisters, to my lady of Bedford, mother to the Queen, and to other ladies noble of this realm . . ."[8]

The inclusion of Jacquetta and Cecily proves that the two women were highly regarded at court, but whether they spoke on the countess's behalf remains unknown. Jacquetta certainly had no reason to help the woman whose husband murdered her own beloved spouse and son. Anne Beauchamp defended herself, saying that she entered sanctuary "for the surety of her person" and not because of any "offence by her done", but she travelled with Warwick to France and stood by his side when he swore his allegiance to Margaret of Anjou and her son.[9] In the end, she might have been guilty of no more than obeying her misguided husband, but she was looked upon as an uncomfortable reminder of the past.

In March 1472, Jacquetta received her own reward for helping her daughter survive during Edward IV's exile. She obtained the "custody of all honours, castles, lordships, hundreds, manors, lands, rents, services, reversions, possessions and other hereditaments and knight's fees, advowsons and appointments of officers" formerly belonging to the late William la Zouche, sixth Baron Zouche and seventh Baron St Maur. She also acquired the wardship of Baron Zouche's son and heir, John, which enabled her to draw profits from his lands. On top of that, she was also rewarded custody of several manors formerly belonging to the family, as well as their lands in various towns. This lucrative grant was an indication that Jacquetta expected to live and enjoy her new privileges, but the duchess died two months later, on 30 May 1472. Had she been terminally ill and not expected to live long, she surely wouldn't have received the grant. It can be thus deduced that Jacquetta's death came unexpectedly, perhaps as a shock to her family. The cause of Jacquetta's death as well as the location of her burial remains unknown. If she composed her last will, and as a widow she was entitled to do so, it didn't survive.

Queen Elizabeth's reaction to her mother's death was not recorded, but there's no doubt she was devastated. Shortly before Jacquetta died, Elizabeth gave birth to her seventh child, a daughter she named Margaret in honour of the King's sister, the Duchess of Burgundy. The infant, born in April, died eight months later. The Queen would give birth to five more children: Richard in 1473, Anne in 1475, George in 1477, Katherine in 1479 and Bridget in 1480.

NOTES

[1] Thomas Wright (ed.), *Political Poems and Songs Relating to English History Composed During the Period From the Accession of Edward III to that of Richard III*, p. 281.

[2] Ibid., p. 278.

[3] Charles Lethbridge *Kingsford, English Historical Literature In The Fifteenth Century*, p. 379.

[4] Ibid.

[5] Norman Davis (ed.), *Paston Letters and Papers of the Fifteenth Century*, Part 1, p. 445.

[6] Ibid., p. 447.

[7] The couple received papal dispensation in April 1472.

[8] Mary Anne Everett Wood, *Letters of Royal and Illustrious Ladies of Great Britain*, Volume 1, pp. 100-104.

[9] Ibid.

CHAPTER 11:
SHADOWS OF THE PAST

Jacquetta didn't live to see the day when the man who was responsible for the unlawful executions of her husband and son was convicted and executed as a traitor. In the late 1470s, George Plantagenet, Duke of Clarence, revived the old claims of Edward IV's alleged bastardy to dethrone him. He also raised doubts about the legitimacy of Edward's children with Elizabeth Woodville, thus challenging the validity of their claim to the throne. The Act of Attainder passed against Clarence stated that he had "falsely and traitorously intended and purposed firmly the extreme destruction and disinheriting of the King's issue".[1] Whether Clarence knew about Edward IV's alleged pre-contract with another woman is open to question, but it's been suggested that he learned about it and thus believed that his brother's children by Elizabeth Woodville were bastards and thus unfit to inherit the crown.[2] Elizabeth Woodville's anxiety about her troublesome brother-in-law was reported six years later by the Italian diplomat Dominic Mancini, who visited England in 1483:

"The queen then remembered the insults to her family and the calumnies with which she was reproached, namely that according to established usage she was not the legitimate wife of the king. Thus she concluded that her offspring by the king would never come to the throne unless the duke of Clarence were removed; and of this she easily persuaded the King."[3]

Writing in the early sixteenth century, Thomas More asserted that "the Queen and the lords of her blood ... highly maligned the King's kindred".[4] The Woodvilles had no reason to speak up for Clarence, who had betrayed Edward IV twice in the past. The Queen may have felt that with Clarence's execution justice had been done. Her father and brother were finally revenged.

In addition to challenging his nephews' rights to the throne, Clarence impugned his mother's chastity yet again. The Act of Attainder stated that George had "falsely and untruly noised, published, and said that the King our sovereign lord was a bastard and not begotten to reign upon us".[5] Cecily Neville's reaction to this remains unclear, but when Edward condemned George to death, she tried to intercede with him on Clarence's behalf. She failed to convince Edward to pardon George, but one contemporary source claimed that she managed to convince the King not to subject his brother to a gruesome death by hanging, drawing and quartering.[6] Instead, George of Clarence was drowned in a barrel of Malmsey wine on 18 February 1478. Two of his children survived him: a daughter, Margaret, and a son, Edward. Margaret would wear a miniature wine barrel on her bracelet to commemorate her father's death.

On 10 November 1480, Queen Elizabeth Woodville gave birth to her tenth and last child by Edward IV. It was another girl, who was named Bridget, an unusual name in England. It's been credibly suggested that Cecily, Duchess of York, chose the name because she cherished a special devotion to St Bridget of Sweden.[7] The baby's name suggests that the royal couple intended to devote this child to God. "My lady the King's mother and my lady Elizabeth", Cecily and Edward IV's eldest daughter, Elizabeth of York, "were godmothers at the font" during the grand christening ceremony. Another godmother, Margaret Beaufort, carried the infant princess beneath a canopy borne by three knights and a baron.[8] Lady Margaret, whose son, Henry Tudor, was still in exile, had recently remarried to Thomas Stanley, a Woodville associate. In the past, she supported the Lancastrians, but she made her peace with the new reigning dynasty and hoped that one day King Edward IV would welcome her son at court.

On 23 May 1482, the royal couple's second daughter, fourteen-year-old Mary of York, died at the Palace of Placentia in Greenwich. Elizabeth and Edward produced healthy children but, as most medieval parents, saw some of them die before reaching adulthood. Mary was their third child who died, after the babies Margaret, who passed away in 1472, and George, in 1479. As the royal line continued through male heirs, Edward IV still had two healthy sons, Edward and Richard, and the succession looked stable albeit it rested on the shoulders of two small boys.

On 25 May 1482, Margaret of Anjou, the former queen of England, passed away in the chateau Dampierre-sur-Loire near Saumur. She had been ransomed by King Louis XI in 1476 and returned to her native France, where she lived out her days in poverty and obscurity. Margaret had relinquished her rights to her Angevin inheritance to Louis XI and died as the guest of Francois de la Vignolles, one of her late father's servants. In her last will, Margaret stated that although she was "sound of mind, reason and thought" she was "weak and feeble of body", hinting at an illness that eventually killed her. Her last wish was to be buried at Angers Cathedral in the tomb of her late parents, René of Anjou and Isabella of Lorraine.[9]

The only valuable possessions Margaret had remaining were her dogs, coveted by Louis XI. The French King wrote to Jeanne Chabot, Madame de Montsoreau, Margaret's friend whose castle stood near Dampierre, requesting his equerry "to bring me all the dogs you have had from the late queen of England." Margaret had made Louis her heir, although she had little or no valuables to bestow upon him. "You know she had made me her heir, and that this is all I shall get", Louis wrote, adding that the dogs were "what I love best". "I pray you not to keep any back, for you would cause me a terribly great displeasure", he urged.[10] In her last will, Margaret mentioned some precious relics she used in private devotions, so she was not entirely stripped of worldly goods, but it was a far cry from what she was expected to have as a former queen.

Had Margaret lived at least a year longer, she would have witnessed Edward IV's death in April 1483 and the accession of his younger brother Richard, Duke of Gloucester. It may have given her comfort to see that the Yorks did, eventually, devour themselves and lost the throne they so brazenly took from her husband.

NOTES

[1] Alison Weir, *Elizabeth of York: The First Tudor Queen*, p. 64.

2 John Ashdown Hill, *The Third Plantagenet: George, Duke of Clarence, Richard III's Brother*, Chapter 13.

3 Dominic Mancini, *The Usurpation of Richard III*, p. 122.

4 George M. Logan (ed.), *The History of King Richard the Third: A Reading Edition*, p. 9.

5 *Rotuli Parliamentorum*, Volume 6, p. 44.

6 J. L. Laynesmith, *Cecily Duchess of York*, p. 145.

7 Alison Weir, *Elizabeth of York: The First Tudor Queen*, p. 70.

8 Ibid., p. 71.

9 Lecoy de la Marche, *Le Roi Rene*, Volume 2, p. 33.

10 Cora Scofield, *The Life and Reign of Edward the Fourth*, p. 159.

CHAPTER 12:
THE END OF AN ERA

On 9 April 1483, Edward IV died after a short illness. He was Cecily Neville's third child who died in adulthood. In recent years, the Duchess of York had lost her daughter Anne, who died in childbirth in 1476, her son George, who was executed in 1478, and now her son the King passed away. Edward was merely forty years old, and his death came as a huge shock both to his family and subjects. Some sources claimed that he died due to overindulgence in food and drink; others even suggested poisoning. Contemporary observer Dominic Mancini reported that the King went fishing and caught a cold. The succession should have devolved upon Cecily's grandson Edward, Prince of Wales, but instead of becoming grandmother to the King, Cecily became, yet again, mother to the King when Richard of Gloucester seized the throne for himself.

Shortly after Edward IV's death, his son, Edward V, set out from Ludlow Castle to London. He was surrounded by his Woodville relatives and their adherents. Among them were Anthony, Jacquetta Woodville's eldest son, and Sir Richard Grey, Elizabeth Woodville's son from her first marriage. Anthony Woodville was Edward V's governor—a supervisor and mentor who took care of the boy's education—and was renowned for his piety, scholarly achievements, military skills and political acumen. Wise and well-read, he sponsored the first-ever published book in England, Geoffrey Chaucer's *The Canterbury Tales*, and in 1477 saw his own translation of *Dicts and Sayings of the Philosophers* printed by William Caxton.

It is notable that in his translation, Anthony omitted some of Socrates's disparaging views of women. Caxton speculated that Anthony did so because of "the very affection, love and good-will that he had unto all ladies".[1] It's tempting to speculate that Jacquetta's careful upbringing contributed to Anthony's chivalric respect of women in an age when most men had no qualms about accepting misogynistic views. Dominic Mancini reported that Anthony was "always considered a kind, serious, and just man, and one tested by every vicissitude of life. Whatever his prosperity, he had injured nobody, though benefitting many; and therefore he [Edward IV] had entrusted to him the care and direction of the King's eldest son".[2]

While Edward V was heading to London, the Duke of Gloucester also set out from his northern estates, surrounded by his servants and one of his new allies, Henry Stafford, the Duke of Buckingham. According to Dominic Mancini, the two parties—one headed by Anthony Woodville and the other headed by Gloucester—decided to meet along the way. Anthony Woodville and Richard Grey rode out to meet with the Dukes of Gloucester and Buckingham in Northampton, leaving Edward V behind in Stony Stratford. The men spent a congenial evening engrossed "in very pleasant conversation".[3]

The next morning, however, Anthony Woodville and Richard Grey were suddenly arrested while the Dukes of Gloucester and Buckingham "hastened at full gallop towards the young King".[4] As the dukes arrived, they arrested more servants who attended Edward V, including Thomas Vaughan, his chamberlain. Both Gloucester and Buckingham exhibited a "mournful countenance, while expressing profound grief at the death of the King's father" and accused Edward IV's ministers of having "little regard for his honour, since they were accounted the companions and servants of his vices, and had ruined his health".[5] Here, the dukes were referring to Edward IV's immoral lifestyle, for he was renowned for his licentiousness.[6] It was common knowledge at court that Edward IV's companions in his wanton behaviour were "three of the aforementioned relatives of the Queen, her two sons and one of her brothers"[7]—Thomas and Richard Grey and Edward Woodville. The dukes, afraid that the same would happen to Edward V, requested that "these ministers should be removed from the King's side". The Duke of Gloucester also accused the said ministers of "conspiring his death and preparing ambushes both in the capital and on the road". Moreover, he said that they attempted to deprive him of the office of regent, which Edward IV had conferred on him, and that he believed himself able to "discharge all the duties of government"[8] because he was more experienced and popular.

The young King replied that he trusted in those men whom his father had given him and that he "had seen nothing evil in them and wished to keep them."[9] Then, Edward V invoked his mother's name, saying that "he had complete confidence in the peers of the realm and the Queen". The Duke of Buckingham, who loathed the Queen's family, angrily retorted that "it was not the business of women to govern kingdoms"[10] and Edward V should relinquish any hope he had in his mother. The young monarch, seeing that his resistance was pointless, had no other choice but to obey the dukes' demands.

When the Queen learned that her son was in the Duke of Gloucester's custody and members of her family were imprisoned, she—together with her second son from her first marriage, Thomas Grey, Marquess of Dorset—tried to raise an army but encountered opposition. Dominic Mancini, who witnessed the events of the spring of 1483 as they unfolded, reported that "when they [the Queen and the Marquess of Dorset] had exhorted certain nobles who had come to the City, and others, to take up arms, they perceived that men's minds were not only irresolute but altogether hostile to themselves".[11]

Without the protection of her royal husband, Elizabeth Woodville was helpless. She must have been shocked when she learned that "some even said openly that it was more just and profitable that the youthful sovereign should be with his paternal uncle [Richard, Duke of Gloucester] than with his maternal uncles and uterine brothers".[12] With her own position fragile, she could not protect the interests of her family. Elizabeth did what had worked once before: she gathered all of her daughters, her son Richard, Duke of York, and, accompanied by the Marquess of Dorset, hurried into the sanctuary of Westminster.

The coronation of Edward V, scheduled for 4 May 1483, never took place. That day, the royal entourage reached London accompanied by the Dukes of Gloucester and Buckingham. They received a heartfelt welcome from the Lord Mayor, aldermen and about five hundred citizens, and, as Mancini claimed, "these two dukes were seeking at every turn to arouse hatred against the Queen's kin, and to estrange the public opinion from her relatives".[13]

The Duke of Gloucester then sent letters to the council claiming that Elizabeth Woodville and her family "have intended and daily doth intend to murder and utterly destroy us and our cousin the Duke of Buckingham and the old royal blood of this realm".[14] Four cartloads of weapons were put in front of Edward V's procession during his entry to London—Gloucester claimed they had been stored by the Woodvilles, who intended to use them against him. Mancini wrote that "many knew these charges to be false"[15] since the weapons had been stored when war was being waged against Scotland.

Having custody of Edward V, Richard of Gloucester started working his own way to the throne. On 7 May, he gathered the executors of Edward IV's last will at Baynard's Castle to debate its contents. Baynard's Castle was Cecily Neville's London residence, and the fact that Richard chose this location as the meeting place points to the possibility that Cecily may have been involved in the events and supported Richard's plans. By 8 May, Richard adopted the title of protector and rescheduled Edward V's coronation to 22 June.

On 13 June 1483, Lord Hastings, Edward IV's close friend and chamberlain, was executed without trial. Then Gloucester convinced Elizabeth Woodville to release her younger son, the Duke of York, and she, persuaded by the Archbishop of Canterbury, who promised that no harm would befall her sons, agreed. Three days later, the Duke of York joined his elder brother in the Tower of London. With his two nephews in his custody, Gloucester quickly made his intentions clear and soon informed the nation that his brother's marriage to Elizabeth Woodville was invalid because of Edward IV's pre-contract to Eleanor Butler.

Eleanor was one of the daughters of John Talbot, first Earl of Shrewsbury, and Margaret Beauchamp. Like Elizabeth Woodville, she was some years older than Edward and was a widow. By the time of Richard III's claim that she was his brother's secret wife, Eleanor was dead and could not confirm his claim; she died in 1468. Eleanor never tried to prove in church courts that her marriage to the King took place and shortly before her death devoted herself to religious life. In Richard III's *Titulus Regius* it was stated that:

"And how also, that at the time of contract of the same pretended marriage, and before and long time after, the said King Edward was and stood married and troth plight to one Dame Eleanor Butler, daughter of the old Earl of Shrewsbury, with whom the same King Edward had made a pre-contract of matrimony, long time before he made the said pretended marriage with the said Elizabeth Grey, in manner and form above said."[16]

Surprisingly, the document doesn't specify when exactly Edward IV secretly married Eleanor, stating only that it took place before he married Elizabeth Woodville. Is there any truth to this? Some historians believe that Richard III fabricated the pre-contract story to bypass his brother's sons and become King, yet it seems inconceivable that he would have invented something that had no basis in truth. Burgundian chronicler Philippe de Commines wrote in his memoirs of how Robert Stillington, Bishop of Bath and Wells, came forward and provided evidence of Edward IV's pre-contract:

"This bishop revealed to the duke of Gloucester that King Edward, being very enamoured of a certain English lady, promised to marry her, provided that he could sleep with her first, and she consented. The bishop said that he had married them when only he and they were present. He was a courtier so he did not disclose this fact but helped to keep the lady quiet and things remained like this for a while. Later King Edward fell in love again and married the daughter of an English knight, Lord Rivers. She was a widow with two sons."[17]

Commines didn't name the woman to whom Edward was pre-contracted, but his very mention of it proves that rumours to that effect certainly circulated in England. Writing in the early sixteenth century, Sir Thomas More asserted that it was not Eleanor Butler but Elizabeth Lucy, mother of Edward IV's illegitimate child Arthur Plantagenet, who was the King's secret wife. Some historians take it to mean that Thomas More was trying to brush Eleanor Talbot out of history, but it's likely that More himself had no knowledge about the identity of the woman who was pre-contracted to Edward IV. How much Cecily Neville knew about her son's pre-contract, if it existed, remains open to question. According to More, at the time of her son's marriage to Elizabeth Woodville, she knew that

Edward IV was pre-contracted to Lady Lucy and arranged for the woman's interrogation, during which Lucy said she was never betrothed to Edward IV.

Some sources state that Richard III's claim to the throne was also based on the assumption that Edward IV himself was a bastard born out of Cecily Neville's adulterous affair. Dominic Mancini wrote that Richard "so corrupted preachers of the divine word that in their sermons to the people they did not blush to say, contrary to heaven's law and religion, that Edward's offspring should be immediately rooted out, because he had not been a legitimate king nor could his descendants be so". The reason was that:

"Edward having been conceived in adultery was wholly unlike the deceased duke of York, whose son he was falsely said to be. But Richard, duke of Gloucester, who most resembled his father, was being called the legitimate successor to the kingdom."[18]

Considering that London was buzzing with rumours at the time, it's possible that Mancini picked up various reports from the past twenty years and conflated them into one narrative. Certainly, gossip about Cecily's alleged adultery and Edward IV's bastardy were circulating in

England during Warwick's first rebellion and at the time of Clarence's execution, and they obviously never died down. Writing after Richard's death, Polydore Vergil stated that Cecily, "being falsely accused of adultery, complained afterwards in sundry places to right many noblemen, whereof some yet live, of that great injury which her son Richard had done her".[19] Cecily referred to these rumours only once during the course of her life. In her last will, she emphasised that Edward IV was her husband's son. Would she have done so if it wasn't true?

On 26 June 1483, Richard was still using Baynard's Castle as his powerbase, and it was there where "all the lords forgathered at the house of Richard's mother" in order to offer him the crown.[20] It's significant that such an important moment in the days leading up to Richard's accession took place at Cecily's property. Again, if he had slandered her reputation, would Cecily allow him to accept the crown at her home?

There are hints that Richard based his claim to the throne not on his brother's alleged bastardy but on the fact that Edward IV's children were illegitimate because of the King's pre-contract that invalidated his marriage to Elizabeth Woodville. In July 1483, Richard referred to

Edward IV as "our dearest brother late king", emphasising at the same time that Edward V was "Edward Bastard late called king Edward V".[21] In January 1484, Richard III's only Parliament enacted the bill known as *Titulus Regius*, which justified his claim to the throne. The bill didn't mention Edward's alleged bastardy but proclaimed Elizabeth Woodville's marriage to Edward IV as an adulterous and unlawful union due to the King's earlier pre-contract. The children born out of this "sinful and damnable adultery" were thus "unable to inherit or to claim anything by inheritance".[22] Furthermore, Elizabeth Woodville was accused of witchcraft and sorcery, and her deceased mother—Jacquetta died in 1472—was named as her accomplice.

On 6 July 1483, Richard of Gloucester was crowned as Richard III. Many people died during his quest for the throne, the most high-profile victims being Anthony Woodville, Earl Rivers, and Richard Grey, Jacquetta Woodville's son and grandson. To Elizabeth Woodville, it was like a flashback of 1469 when the Queen's father and brother were unlawfully executed by Warwick and Clarence. Now yet another member of the York dynasty had executed the Woodvilles. According to *The Crowland Chronicle*, the victims were not accorded a formal trial, although John Rous, also a contemporary observer, recorded that the Earl of Northumberland was their "chief judge".[23] Two days before the executions took place, Anthony Woodville made his last will and wrote a ballad in which he demonstrated that he embraced death. In his last will, Anthony requested "an able priest to pray for the souls of my said Lord my father, my Lady my mother, my brother Sir John, me and all Christian souls".[24] His family was apparently on his mind as he was preparing to meet his Maker.

What Cecily Neville thought of the manner of her son's accession and the deposition of her grandsons remains unknown. Richard III's only surviving letter to his mother during his brief reign was written in June 1484. The wording implies a cordial and warm relationship:

"Madam, I recommend me to you as heartily as is to me possible, beseeching you in my most humble and effectuous wise of your daily blessing to my singular comfort and defence in my need. And madam, I heartily beseech you that I may often hear from you to my comfort. And such news as be here, my servant Thomas Brian, this bearer, shall show to you, to whom please it you to give credence unto. And madam, I beseech you to be good and gracious lady to my lord, my Chamberlain, to be your officer in Wiltshire in such as Colyngbourne had. And that it please you that by this bearer I may understand your pleasure in this behalf. Written at Pontefract the 3rd day of June, with the hand of your most humble son.

Ricardus Rex."[25]

Richard's reign was fraught with difficulties from the very beginning. Shortly after his coronation, a treasonous "enterprise" was undertaken in London; it was a plot to set fires in the city and rescue Edward V and his brother, Richard of Shrewsbury, from the Tower amid general chaos.[26] The Princes in the Tower, as Elizabeth Woodville's sons are known to history, were never seen alive by anyone after the summer of 1483.

What happened to them remains one of history's most compelling mysteries, with murder on Richard III's orders being a possibility. When it was widely circulated in London that the boys were dead, Margaret Beaufort and Elizabeth Woodville hatched a plot together, planning to topple Richard from his throne. Margaret's son, Henry Tudor, was the last living representative of the House of Lancaster, whereas Elizabeth of York, the Dowager Queen's daughter, was the eldest child and heiress of Edward IV.

Together, it was hoped, the two dynasties would be united. Soon Henry Stafford, Duke of Buckingham, joined in with the women. Buckingham's betrayal of Richard III had long puzzled historians—why would he turn on his King and join his enemies? Some suggest that Buckingham learned of Richard's ordering the death of the princes and decided to stake his chances with Henry Tudor. In any case, the Buckingham rebellion, as the uprising is known to history, failed miserably. Buckingham was executed in November 1483, Margaret Beaufort was placed under house arrest and Elizabeth Woodville remained in sanctuary with her daughters, unsure of their futures.

Katherine Stafford, Duchess of Buckingham, the youngest of Jacquetta Woodville's children, was left a widow with two small sons and two daughters. During her husband's rebellion, Katherine was hiding at Weobley Abbey, where she was found by Christopher Wellesbourne, who took her to Richard III. In December 1483, the duchess was allowed to bring her children to London, and by April the King granted her an annuity of £200 per annum.

On 1 March 1484, Richard III solemnly swore that if Elizabeth Woodville and her daughters left sanctuary, no harm would befall them. The former Queen decided to trust

Richard's assertion that she and her children would be in "surety of their lives" and well-provided for and left the sanctuary of Westminster. Her whereabouts after that are unknown; she may have been placed at Heytesbury manor under the watchful eye of her gaoler, Sir John Nesfield, who was paid for her upkeep. Elizabeth of York and her sisters were briefly sent to Richard III's court but joined their mother soon afterwards. The York girls were invited to court for Christmas festivities in 1484, where Elizabeth of York was made much of, wearing the same dresses as Richard III's wife and queen, Anne Neville.

Cecily, Duchess of York, was not resident at her son's court, leading a life of quiet contemplation in her favourite residence at Berkhamsted Castle. The elderly duchess rose at seven, attended morning Mass and had religious books read to her during dinner. She was still an influential figure, as evidenced by the following provision: "After dinner she giveth audience to all such as hath any matter to show unto her by the space of one hour". Then the duchess took a half-hour nap and prayed more when she woke up. During supper, she also listened to religious books and afterwards she "disposed herself to be familiar with her gentlewomen", participating in "honest mirth" with them. One hour before she went to bed, Cecily had a cup of wine and went to her "privy closet", a private chapel attached to her suite, to "take her leave of God for all night, making end of her prayers for that day".[27] By eight o'clock, she retired to bed.

During his brief reign, Richard III lost his son and wife. Edward of Middleham, the King's only legitimate child, died in April 1484 at the age of ten, and his wife passed away on 16 March 1485 during the eclipse of the sun. Soon after Anne's death, Richard was forced to deny rumours that he poisoned her and that he planned to marry his niece Elizabeth of York. On 17 May 1485, Richard travelled from Windsor Castle to stay with his mother Cecily at Berkhamsted. He spent three days there before moving to Kenilworth. It was probably the last meeting between mother and son, as Richard III lost his life during the Battle of Bosworth on 22 August 1485.

Henry Tudor was crowned as Henry VII in the autumn of 1485 and married Elizabeth of York in January 1486. To solidify his union with Elizabeth, Henry had Richard III's *Titulus Regius* repealed, restoring his wife and her family to their former royal dignity. Cecily of York, mother of kings, now avoided any mention of her late son Richard III and gloried in the title of "grandmother of the queen of England".[28] Cecily may have been baffled to observe Henry VII's efforts to canonise his mentally unstable half uncle, Henry VI; he applied to three popes, who responded favourably, but the canonisation was never successfully accomplished. Nevertheless, Henry VI was venerated as a saint, and the royal family was especially devoted to him, as evidenced by the fact that in 1502 Elizabeth of York offered at Henry's shrine at Windsor thrice.[29]

After Richard III's death, Cecily, Duchess of York, went on to live for another decade, witnessing the deaths of her old foes and the births of the new generation of Tudor princes and princesses with Plantagenet blood flowing in their veins. In September 1486, the first Tudor heir, Prince Arthur, was born at Winchester Castle. More Tudor children followed in quick succession: Margaret in 1489, Henry (future Henry VIII) in 1491 and Elizabeth in 1492. The christening of Prince Arthur was one of the first grand ceremonies of the new reign, yet Cecily's presence was not recorded. The Woodvilles, on the other hand, were prominent. Elizabeth Woodville, the Queen's mother, was Arthur's godmother and gave him a richly ornamented golden cup. The prince, dressed in a mantle of crimson cloth of gold furred with ermine, was carried by Elizabeth Woodville's daughter Cecily, who was assisted by Thomas

Grey, Marquess of Dorset, and by John de la Pole, Earl of Lincoln, grandson of Cecily, Duchess of York.

Prince Arthur's christening was the last grand ceremony publicly attended by Elizabeth Woodville. She lived out her days in quiet obscurity at Bermondsey Abbey. Elizabeth's removal from the Tudor court has often been linked to a conspiracy against Henry VII hatched in 1487. During the conspiracy, which started in Ireland, a young boy known as "Lambert Simnel" was recruited to impersonate Edward Plantagenet, Earl of Warwick, the young son of the late George, Duke of Clarence. The pretender was crowned as "Edward VI" and used as a figurehead for rebellion. According to sixteenth-century historian Sir Francis Bacon, Elizabeth Woodville was likely "the principal source and motion" of the rebellion and was thus "banished [from] the world into a nunnery; where it was almost thought dangerous to visit her or see her".[30] Bacon's words have often been taken as historical fact, but in his *History of King Henry VII* he clearly says that he was making conjectures, not stating facts. It would have been strange if Elizabeth opted to depose her son-in-law and grandson and gladly replace them with George of Clarence's son, considering how much she hated George for carrying out her father's and brother's unlawful executions in 1469.

It is more likely that Elizabeth Woodville had nothing to do with the Lambert Simnel conspiracy because she had nothing to gain from it. The person who hoped to gain something and perhaps replace Henry VII on the throne was John de la Pole, Earl of Lincoln. John de la Pole was the son of Elizabeth, Duchess of Suffolk, and thus grandson of Cecily Neville, Duchess of York. Shortly after the christening of Prince Arthur, he left England and joined the court of his aunt, Margaret of York, Duchess of Burgundy. By now Margaret was a childless widow, having lost her husband in 1477, and was a prominent figure on the international political stage. Margaret disapproved of Henry VII because he killed her brother Richard III and toppled the Yorks from the throne. She perceived Henry VII as an upstart and didn't accept that his marriage to Elizabeth of York united the two families. In the words of Polydore Vergil, she was not "mindful of the marriage which finally united the two houses of York and Lancaster. She pursued Henry with insatiable hatred."[31]

Lincoln was designated as Richard III's heir and was perceived by many as a strong contender to the throne, and it is likely that Lambert Simnel was merely a decoy and Lincoln intended to assume the crown. He led an army sponsored by Margaret of York and was slain during the

Battle of Stoke Field on 16 June 1487. This battle is often stated to have been the last battle of the Wars of the Roses.

Polydore Vergil stated that Elizabeth Woodville was placed at Bermondsey Abbey because she made a deal with Richard III in 1484 and left sanctuary, thus endangering Henry VII's cause at the time. Vergil argued that by leaving sanctuary, Elizabeth broke her promise "to those (mainly of the nobility) who had, at her own most urgent entreaty, forsaken their own English property and fled to Henry in Brittany, the latter having pledged himself to her elder daughter, Elizabeth". Chronicler Edward Hall was even sharper in his condemnation of Elizabeth and recorded that her "double doings" endangered Henry's cause at the time.[32]

Yet it was a strange thing to condemn the Dowager Queen for something she did three years earlier. It is more likely that Henry VII planned to seize his mother-in-law's lands to endow his wife. It is also possible that Henry VII desired avoiding the embarrassment of his mother having to defer to the Dowager Queen. Before her son became King, Margaret Beaufort served as Elizabeth Woodville's lady-in-waiting; she was last recorded as carrying Bridget of York, the youngest of Elizabeth's children, to the baptismal font in 1480. The courtly protocol dictated that a crowned Queen should take precedence over other ladies of the court, and Elizabeth Woodville, mother of the current royal consort and herself a crowned Queen, had every right to take precedence over Margaret Beaufort.

There is evidence that Margaret would oppose being superseded by Elizabeth Woodville during court ceremonies. Margaret adopted a semi-regal style and invented the title of My Lady the King's Mother to emphasise her new status. Her manor at Collyweston, which she remodelled, boasted a set of splendidly decorated rooms, one of them being the "Queen's chamber", which she occupied.[33] She also began to use the royal style "Margaret R." instead of the earlier signature "M. Richmond". The *R* stood for "Richmond", as in Countess of Richmond, but it could also be read as "Regina", meaning "Queen" in Latin. Margaret often dressed in sumptuous clothes similar in colour and style to the Queen's and walked beside Elizabeth of York during ceremonies. Henry VII was eager to emphasise that he was King in his own right and not because he was married to the Yorkist heiress; it follows that he would be eager to have his own mother, and not the mother of his wife, prominent at court.

Whatever the reason behind Elizabeth Woodville's retirement, she wasn't forcibly cloistered but allowed to visit court on occasion and treated with the respect of her royal rank. In November 1487, several months after the conspiracy, the King made plans for Elizabeth Woodville to marry King James III of Scotland, and it belies belief that he would have honoured her in this way had she been implicated in a treasonous act only a year earlier. Elizabeth was present at court in May 1489 when the papal envoy reported the opening of the Church's "moneybox", and she also accompanied her daughter the Queen to confinement in October of the same year. In November 1489, she met her kinsman Francis de Luxembourg within Elizabeth of York's chambers. At that time, the royal couple was expecting the birth of their second child, and Elizabeth Woodville was present at her daughter's side when the baby girl, Margaret, was born.

Elizabeth Woodville died on 8 June 1492, a victim of plague, as has been recently discovered.[34] According to her last will, the Dowager Queen had "no worldly goods" to bequeath to "the Queen's Grace, my dearest daughter". She expressed her regret that she could not "reward any of my children, according to my heart and mind" and beseeched God to "bless her Grace, with all her noble issue, and with as good heart and mind as is to me possible, I give her Grace my blessing, and all the aforesaid my children". Elizabeth requested a humble funeral "without pompous entering or costly expenses done thereabout."[35] Her wishes were respected, and she was buried during a low-key ceremony when her body was conveyed from Bermondsey Abbey to Windsor "without ringing of any bells or receiving of the dean or canons in their habits". The herald who recorded the funeral was dismayed at the lack of proper ceremony. The Dowager Queen's hearse was "such as they use for the common people".[36] Historians usually assumed that Elizabeth's low-key funeral was the result of Henry VII's miserliness, yet if she truly died of plague, her body would have been buried as fast as possible and without traditional customs, such as embalming or lying in state for at least two weeks, because it was believed that bodies of plague victims were potential sources of infection.

Shortly after Elizabeth Woodville's death, a new pretender, this time more dangerous than Simnel, appeared on the international political stage of Europe. Perkin Warbeck, as he is known in history, dogged Henry VII's reign and dominated his foreign and domestic politics until his execution in 1499. Like Simnel, he too had the backing of Margaret of York because he claimed to have been

Richard of Shrewsbury, Duke of York, one of the Princes in the Tower, whose fates were still unknown. Margaret claimed that she recognised Warbeck as her nephew, and became one of his staunchest supporters, organising financial aid as well as currying favour with crowned heads of Europe. It's been suggested by some historians that Cecily Neville may have been in contact with her daughter Margaret of York and supported Warbeck's claim because some of her servants were involved in the plot to overthrow Henry VII and crown Warbeck.[37] Yet this theory was debunked by Cecily's recent biographer, who pointed out that Cecily's servants were not as close to the old duchess as previously thought.[38]

Perkin Warbeck's identity is one of the greatest mysteries of history. His claim that he was one of the Princes in the Tower still fuels the debate of what truly happened to Edward IV's sons. Henry VII was adamant that Warbeck was an impostor, and chroniclers of the Tudor reign depicted him as such. Warbeck was later identified by Henry VII as a young man hailing originally from Tournai in Flanders. It's possible that Warbeck was, after all, Cecily Neville's grandson. If his true identity was not that of Richard of Shrewsbury, Duke of York, he may have been either the illegitimate son of Margaret of York or Edward

IV. Contemporaries commented upon the fact that Warbeck resembled Edward IV, and if he was his illegitimate son, that would explain the resemblance.[39]

Whosever Perkin Warbeck was, he didn't have a dramatic impact on Cecily's life. She died a wealthy matron on 31 May 1495. Unlike Elizabeth Woodville, who spent her last years in obscurity at Bermondsey Abbey and died virtually penniless, Cecily had a whole array of goods to bestow to her family and servants, as her last will attests.[40] The most poignant of gifts was given to Prince Arthur, who received, among other things, "a bed of arras of the Wheel of Fortune and tester of the same".[41] Cecily lived her life on the mercy of Lady Fortune, whose images graced tapestries and manuscripts she owned. She tasted triumph and misery, happiness and grief. In the end, she died at the ripe old age of eighty, having outlived her friends and foes by decades. A forceful personality, Cecily made one last statement in her will, proclaiming that she was "Cecily, wife unto the right noble Prince Richard, late Duke of York, father unto the most Christian Prince, my Lord and son King Edward IV".[42] She was no longer highlighting the fact that she felt that she was "queen by right", as it wasn't prudent to do so during the reign of the King who was related to Henry VI, but she was making a loud statement that, despite all the vile rumours, she was always a dutiful and faithful wife. That, perhaps, was what mattered to her the most in the end: that she had once been a wife and mother, even if her husband and sons were no longer among the living.

NOTES

[1] W.J.B. Crotch, (ed.), *The Prologues and Epilogues of William Caxton*, pp. 21-22.

[2] Dominic Mancini, *The Usurpation of Richard III*, p. 69.

[3] The Crowland Chronicle
   http://newr3.dreamhosters.com/?page_id=518

[4] Dominic Mancini, *The Usurpation of Richard III*, p. 77.

[5] Ibid.

[6] Ibid., p. 67.

[7] Ibid.

[8] Ibid., p. 77.

[9] Ibid.

[10] Ibid.

[11] Ibid., p. 79.

[12] Ibid.

[13] Ibid., p. 83.

[14] Arlene Okerlund, *Elizabeth: England's Slandered Queen*, p. 213.

[15] Dominic Mancini, *The Usurpation of Richard III*, p. 83.

[16] *The Parliamentary or Constitutional History of England*, Volume 2, p. 389.

[17] Michael Jones (trans. & ed.), *Philippe de Commynes "Memoirs", 1461-83*, pp. 353-354.

[18] Dominic Mancini, *The Usurpation of Richard III*, p. 94.

[19] *Three Books of Polydore Vergil's English History, Comprising the Reigns of Henry VI, Edward IV and Richard III*, ed. Henry Ellis, pp. 184-185.

[20] Domenico Mancini, *The Usurpation of Richard III*, p. 23.

[21] J. L. Laynesmith, *Cecily Duchess of York*, p. 157.

[22] *The Parliamentary or Constitutional History of England*, Volume 2, p. 390.

23 Keith Dockray, *Richard III: A Source Book*, p. 52.

24 Susan Higginbotham, *The Woodvilles*, p. 181.

25 James Gairdner, *History of the Life and Reign of Richard the Third*, p. 189.

26 Susan Higginbotham, *The Woodvilles*, p. 140.

27 Caroline Halsted, *Richard III as Duke of Gloucester and King of England*, p. 40.

28 J. L. Laynesmith, *Cecily Duchess of York*, p. 169.

29 D. Piroyansky, *Martyrs in the Making: Political Martyrdom in Late Medieval England*, p. 77.

30 Basil Montagu, *The Works of Francis Bacon*, Volume 1, pp. 320, 322.

31 Polydore Vergil, *Anglica Historia*, p. 15.

32 Polydore Vergil, *The Anglica Historia*, p. 19.
Edward Hall, *Hall's Chronicle*, p. 431.

33 E.M.G. Routh, *Lady Margaret: A Memoir of Margaret Beaufort*, p. 77.

34 Euan C Roger, 'To Be Shut Up: New Evidence for the Development of Quarantine Regulations in Early-Tudor England, *Social History of Medicine.*

35 John Nichols, *A Collection of All the Wills*, pp. 350-51.

36 Arlene Okerlund, *Elizabeth: England's Slandered Queen*, pp. 257-59.

37 Ann Wroe, *Perkin: A Story of Deception*, pp. 178-179.

38 J. L. Laynesmith, *Cecily Duchess of York*, pp. 170-171.

39 See more about Perkin Warbeck's identity in Ann Wroe, *Perkin: A Story of Deception,* pp. 517-518.

40 Charles Knight, *London*, Volume 3, p. 11. Elizabeth Woodville, Cecily's once detested daughter-in-law, passed away, a victim of plague, on 8 June 1492.

41 J. Gough Nichols & J. Bruce (ed.), *A Selection From the Wills of Eminent Persons*, pp. 1-6.

42 Ibid.

APPENDIX 1:
THE ORDER OF BIRTH OF JACQUETTA'S CHILDREN

Jacquetta and Richard Woodville had a large number of children, although the exact number remains uncertain; some sources claim there were twelve Woodville children, while others say there were as many as fifteen. Some noble families had manuscripts wherein they entered the order of births of their offspring, but whether the Woodvilles had any such manuscript remains uncertain. The precise dates of the births of Woodville children thus remain unknown, but some can be guessed at based on existing fragmentary evidence. Robert Glover, the Somerset Herald, wrote in the fifteenth century that Jacquetta and Richard had fifteen children. His handwritten note may reflect the order of their births and tallies with other evidence:

"Richard Earl Ryvers and Jaquett Duchess of Bedford hath issue Anthony Earl Ryvers, Richard, Elizabeth first wedded to Sir John Grey, after to King Edward the fourth, Lowys, Richard Erie of Riueres, Sir John Wodeuille Knight, Iaquette lady Straunge of Knokyn, Anne first married to the

Lord Bourchier son and heir to the Earl of Essex, after to the Earl of Kent, Mary wife to William Earl of Huntingdon, John Woodville, Lyonell Bishop of Sarum, Margaret Lady Maltravers, Jane Lady Grey of Ruthin, Sir Edward Woodville, Katherine Duchess of Buckingham."[1]

Anthony was listed in his mother's 1472 inquisition postmortem as being "of the age of thirty years and more," which would put his birth date at around 1442.[2] One document in the *Calendar of the Patent Rolls 1441-1446* states that on 8 June 1446 Jacquetta and Richard had four sons: "Anthony, Richard, John and John".[3] Considering the nature of the document (it was a grant), it's likely to deduce that the boys were listed in the order of their births, thus making it highly likely that Anthony was indeed the eldest child (or the eldest son) born to Jacquetta and Richard. It is somewhat confusing that two of the Woodville sons were christened John, but it was a common practice among medieval nobility to give the same names to different children in case one of them died young. Indeed, one of the Johns did die during childhood. The John who survived was described as being twenty years old in 1465, so he was born around 1445.[4] He later married Katherine Neville, Dowager Duchess of Norfolk, and was executed alongside his father on 12 August 1469. Lionel, who became Bishop of

Salisbury, was said to have been twenty-nine in 1482, so he was born around 1453.[5] The youngest of the Woodville sons was probably Edward, as suggested by the Somerset Herald. Edward's very name suggests that he was born in or around 1453 and named after Margaret of Anjou's son, Edward of Westminster.

Apart from the eight sons born to Jacquetta and Richard, there were also seven daughters. Elizabeth, who became Queen, is usually said to have been the eldest child, born around 1437. This, however, was dismissed by the Woodvilles' recent biographer, who believes that the "date is highly questionable" because it seems to be derived solely from the portrait painted in 1463.[6] According to the highly accurate note of the Somerset Herald, Elizabeth was the eldest daughter, but not the oldest child: Anthony was the eldest, followed by Richard and then Elizabeth. One contemporary document states that Anne was the third daughter, which tallies with the Somerset Herald's note.[7] The youngest Woodville daughter appears to have been Katherine. In her brother Richard's inquisition postmortem in 1492, she was described as being "thirty-four or more", so she was born around 1458.[8] Some sources state that there was also a girl named Martha, who married into the Bromley family, but she doesn't appear in the Somerset

Herald's note or in Richard Woodville's inquisition postmortem in 1492.

In 1469, the Milanese ambassador stated that Elizabeth Woodville "had five brothers and as many sisters", but this statement was incorrect as she had five brothers and seven sisters.[9]

Based on the abovementioned evidence, it appears that Jacquetta and Richard Woodville had fifteen children, two or three of whom died during their childhood. Among them were two Johns and two Richards. Their order of births handwritten by the Somerset Herald is as follows: Anthony, Richard, Elizabeth, Louis, Richard, John, Jacquetta, Anne, Mary, John, Lionel, Margaret, Jane, Edward and Katherine.

NOTES

[1] *Visitations of the North*, p. 58.
[2] TNA: C 140/42/49: Inquisition Post Mortem of Jaquetta de Luxembourg, Late Duchess of Bedford.
[3] CPR 1441-1446, p. 453.
[4] *Annales Rerum Anglicarum*, quoted in Keith Dockray's *Edward IV: A Source Book*, p. 48.
[5] *Calendar of Papal Registers*, Volume XIII, 7 January 1482.
[6] Susan Higginbotham, *The Woodvilles*, p. 14.
[7] *CP*, Volume 5, p. 138.
[8] TNA C 142/7/2: Inquisition Post Mortem of Richard (Woodville, Wydeville), Earl of Ryvers (Earl Rivers): Kent.
[9] *Calendar of State Papers, Milan: 1469*, n. 173.

APPENDIX 2:
THE FATE OF JACQUETTA'S SONS AND DAUGHTERS

As most medieval parents, Jacquetta and Richard Woodville buried at least two or three of their children before they reached adulthood. Infections or childhood diseases may have carried Richard, Louis and John to their early graves. Jacquetta also buried her son John in 1469 after he was executed alongside her beloved husband on the orders of Richard Neville, Earl of Warwick. Anthony, the eldest child, was executed on Richard of Gloucester's orders on 25 June 1483. Anthony, second Earl Rivers, left no legitimate heir to succeed to his earldom, but he had an illegitimate daughter, Margaret, who married Sir Robert Poyntz, lord of the manor of Iron Acton in Gloucestershire. Lionel, Bishop of Salisbury, died by 1 December 1484; the cause of his death remains unknown.[1] Edward, the youngest Woodville son, died in 1488 during the war campaign in Brittany. The earldom of Rivers devolved upon Richard Woodville, who became the third and last Earl Rivers. Richard died in 1491, describing himself in his last will as "the last of the blood", highlighting the fact that he was the last living Woodville male heir.[2] With no son to bestow his title upon, the earldom of Rivers fell into abeyance, and the male Woodville line died out.

Jacquetta, named after her illustrious mother, was married to John Strange, eighth Lord Strange of Knokyn, before March 1450. Her husband died in October 1479 and remarried before that date, which means that Jacquetta died at some point before 1479. Jacquetta and John had only one surviving child, a daughter named Joan, who married George Stanley, son and heir of Thomas, Earl of Derby. Thomas Stanley was married to Margaret Beaufort, mother of Henry VII, and was famous (or perhaps notorious) for changing sides during the Battle of Bosworth, favouring Henry Tudor's claim.

Anne Woodville married William Bourchier, heir of the Earl of Essex, and served as one of her royal sister's ladies-in-waiting during the period from 1466 to 1467, receiving £40 for her services.[3] She may have served Elizabeth longer, but the Queen's household accounts cover only the early part of her queenship. Anne was known at court as Lady Bourchier and never became Countess of Essex, as her husband died in 1480, predeceasing his father. It was Anne's son Henry who became the second Earl of Essex at the age of eleven. Henry was outlived by one daughter, Anne, who became Countess of Essex in her own right upon her father's death in 1540 (he fell from a horse and broke his neck). Anne Bourchier married William Parr and became sister-in-law to Henry VIII's sixth wife. The marriage was miserable, and Anne eloped with her lover, giving birth to two of his children. She died in the 1570s.

Anne Woodville had two more children from her marriage to William Bourchier: Cecily, who married John Devereux, eighth Baron Ferrers of Chartley, and Isabel, who died unmarried. Through Cecily's Devereux marriage, Anne Woodville was the ancestress of Elizabeth I's favourite, Robert Devereux. Following her husband's death, Anne married George Grey, heir of the Earl of Kent. Yet again, she never became a countess, dying in 1489 before her husband succeeded his father as earl. The couple had one son, Richard, who succeeded George as third Earl of Kent. Richard died childless and was succeeded as earl by his half brother Henry Grey, the fourth earl.

Mary Woodville married William Herbert, heir of the Earl of Pembroke, in 1466 and bore him one daughter, Elizabeth. When Mary's father-in-law was executed on 27 July 1469, William succeeded to the earldom of Pembroke, and Mary became a countess. Herbert was later asked by

Edward IV to exchange the earldom of Pembroke for the earldom of Huntingdon, and he agreed. Mary Woodville is perhaps one of Jacquetta's most obscure daughters. The date of her death remains uncertain, but she was dead in 1484 when her husband married Richard III's illegitimate daughter, Katherine Plantagenet.

Margaret Woodville married Thomas FitzAlan, Baron Maltravers, the heir of the Earl of Arundel, in 1464. Thomas succeeded his father as seventeenth Earl of Arundel in 1488, and Margaret became a countess. They had several children; the most prominent among them were William, who succeeded his father as the eighteenth earl of Arundel, Margaret, who married the executed John de la Pole, Earl of Lincoln, and Joan, who married George Neville, fifth Baron Bergavenny.

Joan Woodville married Anthony Grey, son and heir of Edmund Grey, Baron Grey de Ruthyn. Joan's father-in-law received the earldom of Kent in May 1465, but Anthony never succeeded him, dying childless in 1480 and predeceasing his father by ten years. Anthony's younger brother George Grey, who had married Joan's elder sister Mary, became the second Earl of Kent in 1490.

Of Jacquetta's seven daughters, only two were still alive at the time when Richard Woodville, the last Woodville male heir, made his last will in 1491: Elizabeth and Katherine. Elizabeth, Jacquetta's royal daughter, died as a victim of plague in June 1492. Through her daughter Elizabeth of York, she became the ancestress of kings and queens. Through her eldest son of her first marriage, Thomas Grey, Marquess of Dorset, Elizabeth was a great-great-grandmother of Lady Jane Grey, England's "Nine Days' Queen".

Katherine Woodville Stafford, Duchess of Buckingham, remarried in 1485. Her second husband was Jasper Tudor, much-beloved uncle of Henry VII. For years, Jasper held the title of Earl of Pembroke, awarded to him by his half brother, Henry VI, but in the aftermath of his victory at Bosworth, the grateful Henry VII conferred the dukedom of Bedford upon Jasper in recognition of his long service and loyal friendship. Thus on the day of her marriage to Jasper, Katherine succeeded her mother as Duchess of Bedford. Little is known about Katherine and Jasper's life together. During the ten years they spent as a married couple, they didn't produce children. After Jasper's death, Katherine followed in her mother's footsteps and remarried without royal licence; her third and last husband was

Richard Wingfield, who would become a respected ambassador under Henry VIII. Katherine died on 18 May 1497, aged about thirty-nine. She was outlived by four children from her first marriage: Edward, who succeeded his father to the dukedom of Buckingham, Elizabeth, who married Thomas Howard and became Duchess of Norfolk in 1524, Henry, who became Earl of Wiltshire, and Anne, who married Baron Hastings and became one of Henry VIII's first recorded mistresses.

---

[1] Susan Higginbotham, *The Woodvilles*, p. 152.
[2] Ibid., p. 185.
[3] A. R. Myers, *The Household of Queen Elizabeth Woodville, 1466-7*, p. 451.

Picture Section

Figure 1: John of Lancaster, Duke of Bedford, Jacquetta's first husband, as depicted in the *Bedford Book of Hours*, BL Add MS 18850 (source: Wikimedia Commons).

Figure 2: Anne of Burgundy, Bedford's first wife. She commissioned the *Bedford Book of Hours* and presented it to her husband's nephew, Henry VI, on Christmas Eve 1430.

Figure 3: Garter stall plate of Richard Woodville, Earl Rivers, Jacquetta of Luxembourg's beloved second husband (*Stall Plates of the Knights of the Order of the Garter, 1348-1485*, ed. Sir William Henry St John Hope).

Figure 4: Elizabeth Woodville, Jacquetta's eldest daughter, who became Queen consort in 1464 (author's photograph of the portrait).

Figure 5: Cecily, Duchess of York, with her mother and sisters, c. 1435, from a *Book of Hours of Paris Use*, BnF Lat MS 1158 f. 34v (Wikimedia Commons).

Figure 6: Edward IV, son of Cecily Neville, Duchess of York.

Figure 7: Detail from the frontispiece to the *Luton Guild Book 1475-1546*. Kneeling before the Trinity are the founders of the Guild: Thomas Rotherham, Bishop of Lincoln, Edward IV and his wife, Elizabeth Woodville, with immediately behind her the King's mother, Cecily, Duchess of York, one of the few rare representations of her that still exist (Wikimedia Commons).

Figure 8: Kneeling Anthony Woodville, Jacquetta's son, gives his translation of *The Dicts and Sayings of the Philosophers* to Edward IV, Elizabeth Woodville and Edward V (Wikimedia Commons).

Figure 9: Margaret of Anjou and Henry VI in the *Talbot Shrewsbury Book* presented to Margaret on the occasion of her betrothal in 1445. The two noblewomen behind the Queen wear the fashions popular in the 1440s (Wikimedia Commons).

Figure 10: Medal struck by Pietro da Milano c. 1463, showing Margaret of Anjou in her thirties (Wikimedia Commons).

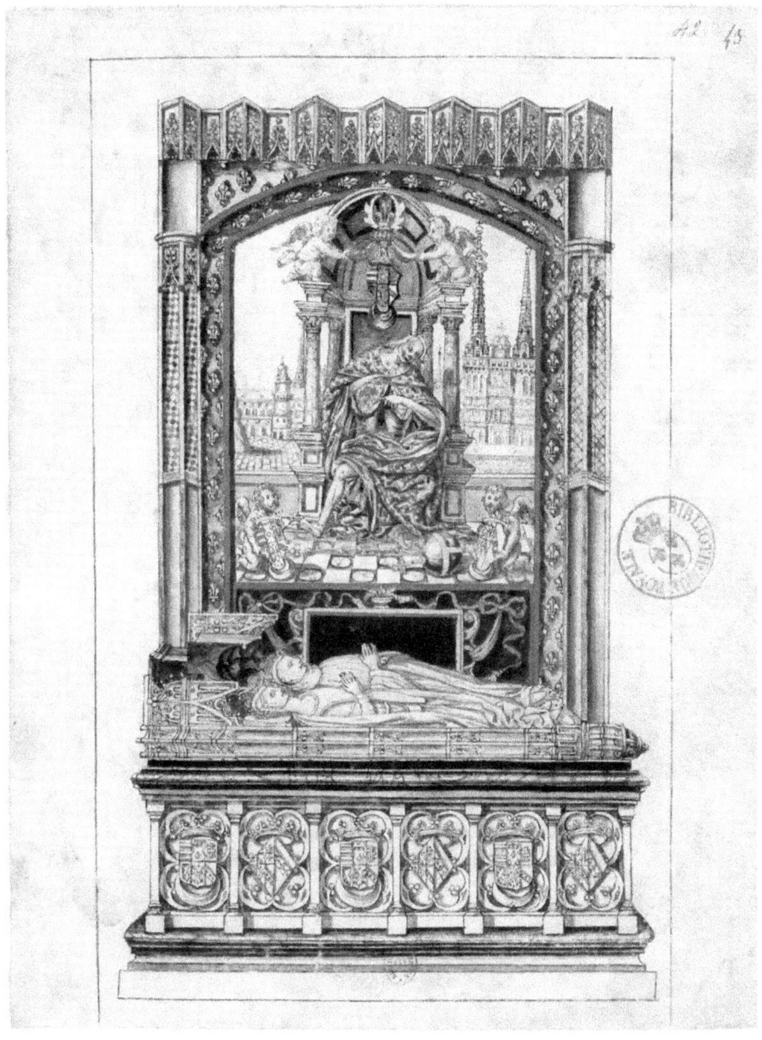

Figure 11: Tomb of Margaret of Anjou's parents, René of Anjou and Isabel of Lorraine, at Angers Cathedral. Margaret's body was interred in their sepulchre, but the tomb was destroyed during the French Revolution, and her remains were not located.

Figure 12: Richard III, Cecily Neville's youngest son.

Figure 13: Elizabeth of York, granddaughter of Jacquetta and Cecily, Queen of England.

SELECTED BIBLIOGRAPHY

Primary Sources: Manuscripts

Christine de Pizan, Collected Works (London: British Library, Harley MS. 4431)

The Bedford Book of Hours (London: British Library, Add. MS. 18850)

The Neville Book of Hours (Paris: Bibliothèque Nationale de France, MS. Latin 1158)

The Salisbury Breviary (Paris: Bibliothèque Nationale de France, MS. Latin 17294)

The Talbot Shrewsbury Book (London: British Library, Royal MS. 15E VI)

Primary Sources: Printed

Blacman, J. *Henry the Sixth: a Reprint of John Blacman's Memoir with Translation and Notes.* Cambridge University Press, 1919.

De Monstrelet, E. *The Chronicles of Enguerrand de Monstrelet.* G. Routledge and Sons, 1867.

De Pizan, Ch. *The Treasure of the City of Ladies: Or the Book of the Three Virtues.* Penguin Books, 2003.

Fabyan, R. *The New Chronicles of England and France.* Ed. Henry Ellis. London, Rivington, 1811.

Froissart, J. *The Ancient Chronicles of Sir John Froissart, of England, France, Spain, Portugal, Scotland, Brittany, and Flanders, and the Adjoining Countries.* J. Davis, 1815.

Hall, E. *Hall's Chronicle: Containing the History of England, During the Reign of Henry the Fourth, and the Succeeding Monarchs, to the End of the Reign of Henry the Eighth, 1548.* Reprint ed., New York: AMS Press, 1965.

Harris, Sir Nicholas, ed. *Privy Purse Expenses of Elizabeth of York: Wardrobe Accounts of Edward IV.* London: W. Pickering, 1830. Reprint ed., New York: Barnes and Noble, 1972.

Mancinus, D. *The Usurpation of Richard the Third,* Trans. C. A. J. Armstrong. 2nd ed. Oxford, Clarendon Press, 1969.

More, T. *The History of King Richard III and Selections from the English and Latin Poems.* Yale University Press, 1976.

More, T. *The History of King Richard the Third: A Reading Edition.* Indiana University Press, 2005.

Vergil, P. *Anglica Historia of Polydore Vergil, A.D. 1485-1537.* The Royal Historical Society, 1950.

Secondary Sources: Books

Ashdown-Hill, J. *The Third Plantagenet: Duke of Clarence, Richard III's Brother.* The History Press, 2014.

Baldwin, D. *Elizabeth Woodville: Mother of the Princes in the Tower.* The History Press, 2010.

Baldwin, D. *Richard III.* Amberley Publishing, 2013.

Breverton, T. *Owen Tudor: Founding Father of the Tudor Dynasty.* Amberley Publishing, 2017.

Crawford, A. *The Yorkists: The History of a Dynasty.* Hambledon Continuum, 2007.

Dockray, K. *Henry VI, Margaret of Anjou and the Wars of the Roses: From Contemporary Chronicles, Letters and Records*. Fonthill Media, 2016.

Gairdner, J. *The Paston Letters, A.D. 1422-1509*. Chatto & Windus, 1904.

Gregory, P., D. Baldwin, and M. Jones. *The Women of the Cousins' War*. Simon & Schuster, 2011.

Gristwood, S. *Blood Sisters: The Women Behind the Wars of the Roses*. Harper Press, 2012.

Higginbotham, S. *The Woodvilles: The Wars of the Roses and England's Most Infamous Family*. The History Press, 2013.

Hollman, G. *Royal Witches: From Joan of Navarre to Elizabeth Woodville*. The History Press, 2019.

Hookham, M. A. *The Life and Times of Margaret of Anjou*. Tinsley Brothers, 1872.

Johnson, L. *Shadow King: The Life and Death of Henry VI*. Head of Zeus, 2019.

Kendall, Paul Murray. *Richard the Third*. Doubleday & Co., 1965.

Laynesmith, J. L. *Cecily Duchess of York*. Bloomsbury Academic, 2017.

Laynesmith, J. L. *The Last Medieval Queens: English Queenship 1445-1503*. Oxford: Oxford University Press, 2004.

Licence, A. *Cecily Neville: Mother of Kings*. Amberley Publishing, 2014.

Licence, A. *Edward IV & Elizabeth Woodville: A True Romance*. Amberley Publishing, 2016.

Licence, A. *Elizabeth of York: The Forgotten Tudor Queen*. Amberley Publishing, 2013.

Licence, A. *Henry VI & Margaret of Anjou: A Marriage of Unequals.* Pen & Sword History, 2018.

Maurer, H. *Margaret of Anjou: Queenship and Power in Late Medieval England.* The Boydell Press, 2003.

Norton, E. *Margaret Beaufort: Mother of the Tudor Dynasty*. Amberley Publishing, 2011.

Okerlund, A. *Elizabeth: England's Slandered Queen.* Gloucestershire, Tempus, 2006.

Pernoud, R. *Joan of Arc: By Herself and Her Witnesses.* Scarborough House, 1990.

Ross, Ch. *Edward IV*. London: Eyre Methuen, 1974.

Taylor, L. J. *The Virgin Warrior: The Life and Death of Joan of Arc*. Yale University Press, 2009.

Stratford, J. *The Bedford Inventories: The Worldly Goods of John, Duke of Bedford, Regent of France (1389–1435).* Society of Antiquaries of London, 1993.

Vale, M. G. A. *Charles VII*. University of California Press, 1974.

Weir, A. *Elizabeth of York: A Tudor Queen and Her World*. Ballantine Books, 2013.

Wolffe, B. *Henry VI*. Methuen London Ltd, 1983.

Secondary Sources: Journal Articles

Charlier, P. et al. "The Embalming of John of Lancaster, First Duke of Bedford (1435 A. D.): A Forensic Analysis". *Medicine, Science and the Law 56, no. 2 (2016): 107-115.*

Freeman, J. "Sorcery at Court and Manor: Margery Jourdemayne, the Witch of Eye next Westminster". *Journal of Medieval History*, 30 (2004).

Gillespie, J. L. "Ladies of the Fraternity of Saint George and of the Society of the Garter", *Albion: A Quarterly Journal Concerned with British Studies*, Vol. 17, No. 3 (Autumn, 1985), pp. 259-278.

Pascual, Lucia Diaz. "Jacquetta of Luxembourg, Duchess of Bedford and Lady Rivers (c. 1416–1472)", *The Ricardian*. 21 (2011).

Sutton, Anne F. and Visser-Fuchs, Livia. "A Most Benevolent Queen: Queen Elizabeth Woodville's Reputation, Her Piety and Her Books". *The Ricardian*. 10 (June 1995): 214 – 245.